IBN BATUTA
IN
THE MALDIVES AND CEYLON

IBN BATUTA
IN
THE MALDIVES AND CEYLON

TRANSLATED FROM THE FRENCH
OF
M. M. DEFREMERY AND SANGUINETTI

ALBERT GRAY

GYAN

Published by

Gyan Publishing House
5, Ansari Road
Daryaganj, New Delhi-110002
Phone: 011-47034999, 9811692060
E-mail: books@gyanbooks.com

Distribution Network
gyanbooks.com
India, USA, Canada, UK, Australia, France

ISBN : 978-81-212-3561-7 (PB)
First Published, Colombo, 1883

2nd Impression 2020

Printed at: Gyan Press, Delhi.

Ibn Batuta in the Maldives and Ceylon
Author: Albert Gray

JOURNAL

OF THE

CEYLON BRANCH

OF THE

ROYAL ASIATIC SOCIETY

1882.

EXTRA No.

EDITED BY THE HONORARY SECRETARY.

" The design of the Society is to institute and promote enquiries into the History, Religion, Literature, Arts, and Social Condition of the present and former Inhabitants of the Island, with its Geology, Mineralogy, its Climate and Meteorology, its Botany and Zoology."

JAMES DUNCAN CAMPBELL, PRINTER,
COLOMBO:

1883.

NOTE

Italics in the text denote the spelling of the French editors: in parentheses, their supplementary explanations. Words and paragraphs within brackets are additions by the translator; as also all foot-notes, except those followed by the initial "*B*," for the insertion of which the Honorary Secretary is responsible.

Errata.

Page 2, 8 lines from bottom, *for* 'Burckhart' *read* 'Burckhardt.'
„ 7, note † *delete 'valu.'*
„ 10, „ † *for 'Haḍégiri' read 'Hadégiri.'*
„ „ „ ‡ *for 'kaptaje' read 'kaptage.'*
„ 12, „ † *for 'fattaru' read 'faṭṭaru.'*
„ 16, „ * *for 'Yúsup' read 'Yúsuf.'*
„ „ „ „ *for 'Tabrij' read 'Tabríz.'*
„ 19, „ ‡ *for 'Mafaï' read 'Máfaĭ.'*
„ „ „ „ *for 'Maáhv' read 'Mahàv.'*
„ 49, „ * *for 'kúdeḷla' read 'kúḍeḷlá.'*
„ 55, „ *for 'Atkalandjeh' read 'Atkalendjeh.'*
„ „ „ * *for 'Dînéwar' read 'Dînéwer.'*

ROYAL ASIATIC SOCIETY

CEYLON BRANCH.

IBN BATU'TA

IN

THE MA'LDIVES AND CEYLON.

[*Translated from the French of M. M. Defrémery and Sanguinetti, by* ALBERT GRAY, M.R.A.S., *late of the Ceylon Civil Service.*]

INTRODUCTION.

THE wonderful travels of Ibn Batúta are a record alike of the commercial activity of the Arabs, and of the far-reaching power of the Bagdad caliphate, whose influence long survived its overthrow. From the swift rise of the Muhammadan power in the seventh century down to the arrival of Vasco di Gama at Calicut in 1498, the trade of Europe with the East was in the hands of the Arabs. The carrying to Europe was done by their ships, but in the Indian seas a vast coast trade was developed by all the nations of the Indian sea-bord—Persians, the races of India, Ceylon, the Eastern Islands and China. After the rounding of the Cape followed in succession the restrictive monopolies of the Portuguese, Dutch, and English, and the Eastern nations have never regained the great and free international commerce of the Arab days.

From the story of Ibn Batúta, one comes to understand how it was possible for a native of Tangiers in the fourteenth century to travel, with but little difficulty, for twenty-four years over every country between Morocco and China. The Muhammadan faith had been spread over a great part of India, and had established a footing in China: Arab merchants were everywhere: and ships were never long in demand for voyages from any one port to any other.

Ibn Batúta was born at Tangiers in 1304, and died at Fez 1377-8. The following summary of his travels of twenty-four years (1325 to 1349) is given by Dr. Birdwood of the India Office. From Tangiers he travelled across Africa to Alexandria, and in Palestine, Syria, and Arabia: down the east coast of Africa to Quilon: across the Indian Ocean to Muscat, Ormuz, Kish, Bahrein and El Catif: through Central Arabia to Mecca and Jeddah: and again in Egypt and Asia Minor, and across the Black Sea to Caffa or Theodosia, and by Azov or Tana 'on past the hills of the Russians' to Bolgar on the Volga—but not daring to penetrate further northwards into 'the land of Darkness.' Returning south to Haj-Tarkhan (Astrakhan) he proceeded in the suite of the wife of the Khan of Kipchah, the daughter of the Greek Emperor Andronicus, westward to Soldaia and Constantiniah (Constantinople), whence returning to Bolgar he travelled on eastward to Bokhara, and through Khorassan to Cabul, Multan, and Delhi where he remained eight years (1334-42). Being sent on an embassy to China he embarked at Kinbaiat (Cambay), and after many adventures at Calicut (where he was honorably received by the 'Samari' or Zamorin) and Hunawar (Onore), and in the Máldive Islands (beginning of 1343—August, 1344) and Ceylon and Bengal, he at last took his passage toward China in a junk bound for Java, as he calls it, but in fact Sumatra. Returning from China, he sailed direct from the coast of Malabar to Muscat and Ormuz: and travelling by Shiraz, Bagdad, Jerusalem, Damascus and for the fourth time to Mecca, Egypt, Tunis, at last reached Fez again, after an absence of half his life-time. Subsequently he spent six years in Spain and Central Africa, where he was the guest of the brother of a countryman of his own from Ceutra, whose guest he had been in China. "What an enormous distance lay between these two!" he exclaims.

The first detailed account of his book was published in Europe only in 1808. Moura in 1845 commenced a translation in Portuguese of a copy obtained at Fez at the end of last century. The abridgment translated by Lee was brought from the east by Burckhart. It was not till the French conquest of Algeria that the best and completest texts were obtained. Five are in the Imperial Library at Paris, only two of which are perfect. From these M. M. Defrémery and Sanguinetti made their translation for the Societé Asiatique: and it is from their version that the present account of the Máldives and Ceylon visit has been extracted. His description of the Máldives is the most interesting and complete in existence, excepting only that of Pyrard de Laval.

IBN BATUTA
IN
THE MALDIVES AND CEYLON.*

I RESOLVED to go to the *Dhîbat Almahal* (*the Máldives*) of which I had heard much. Ten days after we had embarked at Calicut we arrived at the *Dhîbat Almahal* islands. *Dhîbat* is pronounced as the feminine of *Dhîb* (*Arabic for "wolf": it is really an alteration of the Sanskrit* douîpa, "*island*"). These islands are among the wonders of the world: they number about 2,000.† A hundred or less of these islands lie together in a circle in the form of a ring: the group has an entrance as to a harbour, and ships get through by that alone. When a ship arrives near one of these islands it must of necessity have a pilot from among its natives, so that it may reach the other islands under his guidance. They are so close to each other that the tops of the palms which grow on one seem to belong to its neighbour.‡ If the vessel misses its way it cannot reach the islands, and is driven by the wind to *Ma'bar* (*coast of Coromandel*) or towards Ceylon.

---

* *Voyages d'Ibn Batoutah*, par C. Defrémery et Le Dr. B. R. Sanguinetti, Tome IV., 110—185, 191–2, 205–6, 207–10. Paris, 1879.

† See Gray, J. R. A. S., 1878, Vol. X. N. S., pp. 196–7, notes 2, 3; and "The Máldive Islands" (Ceylon Sessional Papers, 1881), pp. 3, 4, 5, Notes (1) (6)—*B.*

‡ So too more recent travellers:—"The Malabares say that heretofore they were joyn'd to the Continent, and were separated by the sea, which in some places hath left such narrow divisions that an active man might leap from one side to the other" (*Mandelso's Travels into the Indies*, 1639. Lib. II. 116. London, 1662). "But that which makes them so numerous is the multitude of canals that divide them; which are so narrow that the sprit-sails of the ships strike the leaves of the trees which are planted on both sides. And in some places a nimble man may leap into an island from the top of a bough that grows in another."—(*Collection of Voyages of the Dutch East-India Company*, p. 131. London, 1703)—*B.*

All the inhabitants of these islands are Musalmáns, pious and honest people. They are divided into regions or zones, each of which is ruled by a governor called *Cordoûiy.* Among these zones the following are distinguished: (1) the zone of *Pâlipour;* (2) *Cannaloûs;* (3) *Mahal,* the province after which all the islands are called, and at which their sovereigns reside; (4) *Téládib;* (5) *Caraïdoû;* (6) *Teïm;* (7) *Télédommety;* (8) *Hélédommety,* the name differing from the preceding only by having its first letter an *h:* (9) *Béreïdoû;* (10) *Candacal;* (11) *Moloûc;* (12) *Souweïd.* The last is the most distant of all.* All the Máldive islands are destitute of grain, except that in the province

* The French editors identify these names with those given by Pyrard as follows:—"*Pâlipour*—'Padypolo': *Mahal*—'Malé': *Caraïdoû*—'Caridou': *Télédommety*—'Tilla dou matis': *Hélédommety*—'Milla doue madoue': *Béreïdoû*—'Poulisdous': *Moloûc*—'Molucque': *Souweïd*—'Souadou.' The *Cannaloûs* of Ibn Batúta, they add, is perhaps the 'Collomadous' of Pyrard, or, as Horsburgh writes it, 'Colomandous.

["The majority of the above 'are easily recognisable,' but five (viz., *Cannaloûs, Téládib, Teïm, Hélédommety,* and *Candacal)* present more difficulty,—some, indeed, being shaped, *more Arabico,* out of all but unsatisfactory conjectural recognition.

"As regards *Hélédommety,* the French translators would appear to be at fault. It may perhaps with more reason be taken as equivalent to *Heladu(m)-matí* (S. *hela,* 'white,' or even *sela,* = Jav. *sela,* 'rock' + *dúva,* 'island' + *matu-piṭa,* 'above') passing by contraction into *Had-dummati. Aḍḍú* may similarly be a contracted form of *Hela-dú* or *Hulu-dú*—the name of one of the islands in that Atol.

"If it be open to question the orthography of the MS. and, supposing an error of the copyist, read *Néládíb* for *Téládíb*—*t* and *n* are not unlike in Arabic—it can be at once fitted to *Nilandu* Atol. Even accepting the received form as correct, the identification may possibly be not considered too far-fetched. Cf. *Tojaree* = ? *Nausâri; Accanee* and *Kaluftee* islands' (Lakkadive group) = *Aucutta, Kalpeni.* Adm. Chart. (Col. Yule in Indian Antiquary, Vol. III., pp. 212-4 on "Names in the *Tohfat-al Majâhidin.*")......

"To attempt to twist the rest into probable coincidence with the modern names of the remaining Atols seems hopeless. But the identification of *Caraïdoû* with *Caridou* (*Kaharidú*)—if accepted—suggests a likely clue to their origin. Admitting that this island—now-a-days of comparative insignificance

of *Souweïd* there is a cereal like the *anly (a kind of millet)* which is brought thence to *Mahal.** The food of the natives consists of a fish like the *lyroûn*, which they call *koulb almâs.* Its flesh is red: it has no grease, but its smell resembles that of mutton. When caught at the fishing, each fish is cut up into four pieces, and then slightly cooked: it is then placed in baskets of coco leaves and suspended in smoke. It is eaten when perfectly dry. From this country it is exported to India, China and Yaman. It is called *koulb almâs*† (cobolly masse, *i.e.,* "*black fish*" *according to Pyrard, Part 1, p. 210, 214.*)

—was of sufficient importance in the 14th century to be classed as a 'province', it is not improbable that other islands would have been taken as representative of whole groups or Atols.

"*Téládib*, if not *Nilandu*, might then be *Toḍḍu*, on the analogy of *Haddummati* from *Hélédomméty: Cannaloûs—Kinaḷos*, 'Kenoorus,' Admiralty Chart, (Máḷosmaḍulu Atol): *Candacal—Kedikoḷu*, 'Kaindecolu,' Admiralty Chart, (Miladummaḍulu Atol. *Cannaloûs* and *Teïm* should lie *North* of Málé. Ibn Batúta, crossing from the Malabar coast, landed first at the former, 'an island fair to behold, where there are many mosques,' and touched later at *Teïm* 'after four days' cruise' when bound for *Mahal* (Málé)."—(*The Máldive Islands*, p. 18, Note (1), Ceylon Sessional Papers, 1881.)

Colonel Yule and Mr. Gray identify *Teïm* with *Utímu* (Admiralty Chart, *Oteeim*) near north end of Tiladummati Atol. "*Cannalous, Candecal* and *Otimo* appear in the oldest European maps"—*B.*]

* Either the fine grain known to the Siṉhalese as (i.) *tana hál (Setaria Italica)*, M. *urá* (Pyrard, *oura*), or (ii.) *menéri* (*Panicum miliaceum*), M. *kudibai*—both of which are found on the Southern Atols. Some nacheri or *kurakkan* (*Cynosurus corocanus*), M. *bimbi* (Pyrard, *bimby*), is grown on the Northern Atols—*B.*

† *Koulb almâs*:—Pyrard has *cobolly masse* (Pyrard, third edition, 1619, p. 210), and *combolly masse* (p. 214), and says the words mean "black fish." See also Pridham 'Ceylon', p. 605. The Siṉhalese call it *umbalakaḍa.* [See "Note on Fish-curing at the Máldives" (Ind. Ant., July, 1882, Vol. XI., pp. 196-8):—"The real 'Máldive fish' (M. *kaḷubili mas*, vulgarly *komboli mas*), S. *umbala kaḍa*) of the Ceylon and Indian markets are chiefly *bonito* (S. *balayá*) –Scomber Pelamis, *Linn.*" *Kaḷubiḷi=kaḷu*, 'black' : *bili* (S. *balayá*,) 'bonito.' —*B.*]

The Trees of the Máldives.

Most of the trees on these islands are coconuts: they furnish the food of the inhabitants along with the fish, of which mention has been made. The nature of the coconut is marvellous. One of these palms produces each year twelve crops, one a month. Some are small, others large: many are dry [yellow], the rest are green and remain always so. From the fruit is obtained milk, oil, and honey, as we have said in the first part of this book. With the honey is made pastry, which they eat with the dried coconut. All the food made from the coconut, and the fish eaten at the same time effect an extraordinary and unequalled vigor in manhood. * * * *

Among the remarkable trees of these islands are the *tchoumoûn* (*Eugenia Jambu*) the lemon, the lime and the colocasia. From the root of the last named, the natives prepare a flour with which they make a kind of vermicelli, and this they cook in coco milk; it is one of the most agreeable dishes in the world. I had a great taste for it and ate it often.*

Of the Inhabitants of these Islands and some of their Customs: Description of their Dwellings.

The inhabitants of the Máldive islands are honest and pious people, sincere in good faith and of a strong will: they eat only what is lawful, and their prayers are granted. When one of them meets another, he says "God is my lord: Muhammad is my prophet: I am a poor ignorant being." In body they are weak and have no aptitude for combat or for war, and their arms

* "The island [Málé] produces .... a bulb in shape and appearance much resembling an ordinary potatoe, but having a pungent flavor. This the natives grate down, and steep in water for some time to deprive it of the unpleasant taste, and dry it afterwards, when it looks very much like flour, and is very palatable" (Christopher and Young in Trans. Bombay, Geographical Society, 1836-38, p. 80). Without doubt the yam called by Máldivians *hittala* (Pyrard, *itelpoul*, "an edible root which grows in abundance, round and large as the two fists") and probably identical with the *hiritala (Dioscorea oppositifolia)* of the Siṇhalese—*B.*

are prayers. One day in this country, I ordered the right hand of a robber to be cut off; upon which many of the natives in the hall of audience fainted away. The Indian pirates do not attack them, and cause them no alarm, for they have found that whoever takes anything of theirs is struck with a sudden calamity. When a hostile fleet comes to their shores, they seize what strangers they find, but do no harm to the natives. If an idolater appropriates anything, if it be but a lime, the chief of the idolaters punishes him and beats him severely, so much does he fear the results of such an action. Were it otherwise, certainly these people would be a most contemptible foe in the eyes of their enemies, because of the weakness of their bodies. In each of their islands there are fine mosques, and most of their buildings are of wood.

The islanders are good people: they abstain from what is foul, and most of them bathe twice a day, and properly too, on account of the extreme heat of the climate and the abundance of perspiration. They use a large quantity of scented oils, such as sandal-wood oil, &c., and they anoint themselves with musk from *Makdachaou.** It is one of their customs, when they have said the morning prayer, for every woman to go to meet her husband or son with the collyrium box, rose-water and musk oil He smears his eye-lashes with collyrium, and rubs himself with rose-water and musk oil, and so polishes the skin and removes from his face all trace of fatigue.

The clothing of these people consists of cloths. They wrap one round their loins in place of drawers, while on their backs they wear the stuffs called *alouilyân* † which resemble the *ihrâm*

* *Makdachaou* :—? Madagascar. [Rather *Magadoxo* on the Zanzibár coast, which Ibn Batúta had visited (Tome II., 181.) "After leaving Zaila we sailed on the sea for fifteen days, and arrived at *Makdachaou* an extremely large town."—See Yule's Marco Polo. Vol. II., p. 347—*B.*]

† *Alouilyân—ouilyân* (p. 120) :—A probable corruption of M. *féliya*, (cf : S. *valu*, *pili*, 'clothes') the term for the *kambaya* (S) or waist cloth worn by Máldivian women commonly and by soldiers on special occasions. The Maldive equivalent for the *ihrâm* is known as *digu libás—B.*

(clothes worn by the Musalmáns during the pilgrimage). Some wear the turban, others supply its place with a little kerchief. When any one meets the *Kâdhi* or the preacher, he takes his garment off his shoulders, and uncovers his back, and so accompanies the functionary till he arrives at his place of abode. Another of their customs is this—when one of them marries, and goes to the house of his wife, she spreads cotton cloths from the house door to that of the *(nuptial)* chamber: on these cloths she places handfuls of cowries on the right and left of the path he has to follow, while she herself stands awaiting him at the door of the apartment. On his arrival she throws over his feet a cloth which his attendants take up. If it is the wife* who goes to the husband's house, that house is hung with cloths, and cowries are placed thereon: and the woman on her arrival throws the cloth over his feet. And this is also the custom of the islanders when they salute the sovereign, they must without fail be provided with a piece of cloth to cast down at the moment, as we shall hereafter describe.

Their buildings are of wood† and they take care to raise the floor of their houses some height above the ground, by way of precaution against damp, for the soil of their islands is damp. This is the method they adopt: they cut the stones, each of which is of two or three cubits long, and place them in piles then they lay across these beams of the coco-tree, and afterwards raise the walls with boards. In this work they show marvellous skill. In the vestibule of the house they construct an apartment which they call *mâlem*,‡ and there the master of the house

---

* It appears from this passage that the two kinds of Siṇhalese marriage, *bína* and *diga*, were in vogue at the Máldives. [Both forms are said to be recognised still—*B*.

† Even at the present day there is but *one* stone or brick built private house at Málé (Sultan's Island)—*B*.

‡ *Mâlem.* "A partition near the middle divides the house into two rooms, one of which is private, and the other open to all visitors." (Trans. Bombay Geographical Society, 1836-8, p. 59.) The public room is called *béru-gé* and the private or women's apartment *eteri-gé*, or in the Southern Atols *mával-gé*—*B*.

sits with his friends. This room has two doors, one opening on the vestibule by which strangers are introduced, the other on the side of the house by which the owner enters. Near the room in question is a jar full of water [? and] a bowl called *ouélendj** made of the coconut shell. It has a handle of [only] two cubits, wherewith to draw the water from the wells, by reason of their little depth.

All the inhabitants of the Máldives, be they nobles or the common folk, keep their feet bare. The streets are swept and well kept: they are shaded by trees, and the passenger walks as it were in an orchard. Albeit every person who enters a house is obliged to wash his feet with water from the jar placed near the *mâlem,* and rub them with a coarse fabric of *lîf*† *(stipulæ which envelope the base of the stalks of the date-palm leaves)* placed there: after which he enters the house. Every person entering a mosque does the same. It is a custom of the natives when a vessel arrives for the *canâdir (in the singular* cundurah*)* ‡ *i.e.,* the little boats to go out to meet it, manned by the people of the island and bearing some betel and *caranbah* § that is to say, green coconuts. Each presents some of these to whom he will of those on board the ship, and then becomes his host carrying to his own house the goods belonging to him, as if he were one of his near relations. Any one of the new-comers who wishes to marry, is at liberty to do so. When the time comes for his departure, he repudiates his wife, for the people of the Máldives do not leave their country. As for a man who does not marry,

---

* *Ouélendj* :—These cocoanut bowls with long handles (M. *dáni,* but cf: S. *valanda* "chatty") are regularly used by the Islanders for drawing water The ordinary cocoanut ladle or spoon they call *uduli.—B.*

† *Lîf* :—Pers.—*B.*

‡ *Canâdir, cundurah* :—The old Portuguese historians speak of Máldive "*gundras,*" and the term is still commonly applied in Ceylon to these Islanders (e. g., S. *Gundara-kárayó*) and their boats (M. *dóni, odi*).—See too C. A. S. Jour. No. 24, p. 135, 1881.—*B.*

§ *Caranbah* : = S. *kurumba* [M. *kuruba.—B.*]

the woman of the house in which he is lodged prepares his food, serves it, and supplies him with provisions for his journey when he goes. In return she is contented to receive from him a very small present. The revenue of the treasury, which is called *bender* *(*custom-house*) consists in the right of buying a certain portion of all cargo on board ship, at a fixed price, whether the commodity be worth just that or more : this is called the *bender* law. The *bender* has in each island a house of wood called *bédjensâr* where the governor, the *cordouéry*, (*above it is written* cordoûiy)† collects all such goods : he sells or barters them. The natives buy with chickens any pottery which may be brought : a pot fetches five or six chickens.

Ships export from the islands the fish of which I have spoken, coconuts, fabrics, the *ouliyân* and turbans : these last are of cotton. They export also vessels of copper, which are very common there, cowries‡ and *kanbar*§, such is the name of the

---

* *Bender:*—See Pyrard, p. 231, "*bandery*": cf. Sin. *banḍhára.* The system of raising revenue here described was still in force in Pyrard's day (Pyrard, chap. xvii.), and seems to be identical in principle with the 'culture system,' employed by the Dutch in Java, where it is supposed to have been invented by one of the Dutch governors subsequent to the English occupation. [Each Atol has its own storehouse (*váru-gé*) into which the revenues of the Sultan are received, and whence they are transferred from time to time to the Treasury (*boḍu baḍéri-ge*, cf : S. *bhánḍágárika*) at Málé.—*B.*]

† *Cordouéry, cordoûiy* :—"The Atol-wari [*Atoḷu-veri* or *Váru-veri*; Pyrard '*varuery*'] is a governor or chief of a division of islands called an Atol ...... It is his duty to collect the revenue of the Atol, and to transmit it to the Hindeggeree [*Haḍégiri*]...... The Rarhu-wari [*Rarhu-veri*] or headman of an island, stands in the same relation to the Atol-wari, as the latter does to the Hindeggeree, in respect to the revenue." (*Trans. Bombay Geo. Soc.*, 1836-8, p. 72).—*B.*

‡ *Cowries* :—'Ibn Baṭúṭa calls them *wada*' [Ar.], and the Two Muhammadans of the 9th century *kaptaje* : Pyrard, *bolly* or *bollis* : Christopher [correctly] *boli*, cf : S. *bella.*

§ *Kanbar* :—Ar. Pyrard has *cairo* (= T. *kayiru*, Gray.) The proper Máldive term *rónu* = S. *réna.* It is hard to believe that "vessels of copper" ever formed one of the genuine exports from the Máldives. A few old copper pots are occasionally sent over to Ceylon for repair.—*B.*

fibre which envelopes the coconut. The natives make it undergo a preparation in pits dug near the shore: then they beat it with picks, after which the women work it into rope. They make of it cord for joining the boards of their ships, and such cordage is exported to China, India and Yemen. *Kanbar* rope is worth more than hemp. With this cord the *(boards of)* ships are joined in India and Yemen, for the Indian sea is full of rocks, and if a ship joined with iron bolts strikes a rock, it is broken up: but when it is fastened with this cord it has elasticity, and does not break.

The money of the islanders consist of cowries. This is the name of a creature *(a mollusc)*, collected in the sea and placed in pits dug out on the beach. Its flesh decays and there remains only the white shell. A hundred of these shells is called *syâh*, and 700, *fâl*; 12,000 are called *cotta*, and 100,000 *bostoû*. Bargains are struck through the medium of these cowries, at the rate of four *bostoû* to a dînâr of gold. Often they are of less value, such as twelve *bostoû* to a dînâr.* The islanders sell them to the people of Bengal for rice, for they too use them for money. They are sold in the same way to the people of Yemen, who use them for ballast in their ships in place of sand. These cowries serve also as a medium of exchange with the negroes in their native country. I have seen them sold, at *Mâly* and at *Djoudjou*, at the rate of 1,150 to a *dînâr* of gold.†

THE WOMEN OF THE MÁLDIVES.

The women of these islands do not cover the head: the sovereign herself does not so. They comb their hair and tie it

* *Syâh* = Sin. *siya.* Ibn Batúta says *bostoû* = 1 dinâr of gold [= about 10 shillings, Lane], and Pyrard says 12,000 = 1 *larin* = 8 *sols.* [Cowries are usually sold in the Islands by the *hiya* = 100, the *falé* = 800 to 1,000, and the *koṭṭé* = 12,000 *(bára-fá.)* A *koṭṭé* is not now worth more than Rs. 1 at Málé.—*B.*]

† *Mâly*; *Djoudjou*:—Two places in the Soudán, afterwards visited by the traveller.

up on one side [of the head.] Most of them wear only a cloth, covering them from the navel to the ground: the rest of the body remains uncovered. In this costume they promenade the bazárs and elsewhere. While I was invested with the dignity of Kází in these islands, I made efforts to put an end to this custom, and to compel the women to clothe themselves: but I could not succeed. No woman was admitted to my presence in the trial of a case, unless she had her whole body covered: but, saving that, I had no power over the usage.* Some women wear, besides the cloth, chemises with short and full sleeves. I had some young female slaves whose dress was the same as that of the women of Delhi. They covered the head: but that disfigured rather than embellished their appearance, as they were not used to it.

The ornaments of the Máldive women consist of bracelets: each has a certain number on both arms, indeed, so that the whole of the arm from the wrist to the elbow is covered. These trinkets are of silver: only the wives of the Sultan and his nearest relatives wear bracelets of gold. The Máldive women have also *khalkhâl (anklets)* called by them *bâïl*, and collars of gold round the neck, called *besdered.*† One of their curious customs is to engage themselves as house servants, in consideration of a fixed sum, which does not exceed five pieces of gold. Their board is at the expense of those who hire them. They do not regard this as a disgrace, and most of the daughters of the inhabitants do it. You will find in the house of a rich man ten or twenty of them. The cost of all dishes broken by one of these maids is charged against her. When she wishes to go from one house to another, the masters of the latter give her the amount of her debt, this she remits to the people of the house she is

---

* Pyrard, 3rd ed., pp. 82, 124, says that all women in his time carefully kept the breasts covered. [A more modern innovation is the adoption by the women on most Atols of a head kerchief.—*B.*]

† (i) *Khalkhâl,* Ar. (ii) *bâïl,* cf: M. *fá* 'leg,' *fiyavaḷu* 'foot,' *takahoḷi* 'anklet'; (iii) *besdered* = M. *fattaru* 'necklace'.—*B.*]

leaving, and her new masters become her creditors.* The principal occupation of these hired women is to rope the *kanbar* (*vide supra.*)

It is easy to get married in these islands, owing to the smallness of the dowry, as well as by reason of the agreeable society of the women. Most of the men say nothing about a nuptial gift, contenting themselves with declaring their profession of the Musalmán faith, and a nuptial gift in conformity to the law is given. When ships arrive, those on board take wives, and repudiate them on their departure : it is a kind of temporary marriage. The Máldive women never leave their country. I have never seen in the world women whose society is more agreeable. Among the islanders, the wife entrusts to no one the care of her husband's service : she it is who brings him his food, takes away when he has eaten, washes his hands, presents the water for his ablutions, and covers his feet when he wills to go asleep. It is one of their customs that the wife never eats with her husband, and that he does not know what his wife eats. I married in that country many wives : some ate with me at my request : others did not, and I could not succeed in seeing them take their food, and no ruse to get a sight was of any avail.

THE STORY OF THE MOTIVE FOR THE CONVERSION OF THE INHABITANTS OF THESE ISLANDS TO ISLÁM : DESCRIPTION OF THE EVIL SPIRITS WHO WROUGHT HARM TO THEM EVERY MONTH.

Trustworthy men among the inhabitants, such as the

* Regarding these servants (M. *femuséri*), who are still employed, Mr. Gray (J. R. A. S., Vol X., N.S., p. 204) has the following note:—" *Pemousseré* [Pyrard, p. 225] 'bondsmen on loan,' debtors who have to serve their creditor till they pay. They are generally well treated and fed; if not they are entitled to their freedom. 'Many a poor man voluntarily enters the service of some great lord as a *pemousseré* to gain his protection and favour.' Christopher says that the men of Malé having to pay no taxes are very lazy and 'become dependents of any of the chiefs, most of whom retain as many followers as they may be able to support, a large retinue being a sign of rank and power.' Compare with this custom the growth of the feudal system in the West."—*B.*

juris-consult *Iça Alyamany*,* the juris-consult and schoolmaster *'Aly*, the Kází *'Abd Allah*, and others, related to me that the population of the islands used to be idolaters, and that there appeared to them every month an evil spirit from among the Jinn, who came from the direction of the sea. He resembled a ship full of lamps. The custom of the natives, as soon as they perceived him, was to take a young virgin, to adorn her, and conduct her to a *boudkhânah*,† *i. e.*, an idol temple, which was built on the sea shore and had a window by which she was seen. They left her there during the night and returned in the morning: then they found the young girl dishonored and dead. They failed not every month to draw lots, and he upon whom the lot fell gave up his daughter. At length arrived among them a Maghrabin‡ called *Abou'lbérécât*, the Berber, who knew by heart the glorious Kurán. He was lodged in the house of an old woman of the island *Mahal*. One day he visited his hostess and found that she had assembled her relatives, and that the women were weeping as if they were at a funeral. He questioned them upon the subject of their affliction, but they could not make him understand the cause. An interpreter coming in informed him that the lot had fallen upon the old woman and that she had one only daughter, who had to be slain by the evil Jinní. *Abou'lbérécât* said to the woman:

* *Iça Alyamany*:—i. e., ? *Isá Falliyá Maniku*. The *Falliyá Maniku* is the Sultan's Secretary and Keeper of the Privy Seal.—*B.*

† *Boudkhânah*:—It is very probable that this was a Buddhist temple. Christopher gives *buḍu* as the modern Máldive for "image" (J. R.A.S., Vol. VI., o.s., p. 57). But the word *bodd* seems to have been a general term for an image with the Arab Oriental travellers, and may only indicate that the Buddhist parts of India were the first visited by the Arabs.—*Journ. As*, 1845, p. 167. Ibn Batúta elsewhere says that the Jama Masjid of Delhi was built upon the sight of a former *Boudkhânah* he does not therefore mean to imply that the word was Máldive. [For some remarks on "Buddhism at the Máldives" see Ceylon Sess. Pap., 1881, 'The Máldive Islands.'—*B.*]

‡ *Maghreb*:—The name given by the Arabs to the Moorish principalities of North-west Africa, nearly corresponding with what we now call Morocco.

"I will go to night in thy daughter's stead." At that time, he was entirely beardless. He was conducted the night following to the idol temple after he had done his ablutions. There he set himself to recite the Kurán, then by the window he perceived the demon, and continued his recitation. As soon as the Jinní came within hearing of the Kurán, he plunged into the sea; and when the dawn was come, the Maghrabin was still occupied in reciting the Kurán. The old woman, her relatives and the people of the island came to take away the girl, according to their custom, and to burn the corpse. They found the stranger reciting the Kurán, and conducted him to their King, by name *Chénoûrâzah,** whom they informed of this adventure. The King was astonished: the Maghrabin proposed to him to embrace Islám, and inspired him with a desire for it. Then said *Chénoûrâzah* to him:—"Remain with us till next month, and if you do again as you have just done and escape the evil Jinní, I will be converted." The stranger remained with the idolaters and God disposed the heart of the King to receive the true faith. He became Musalmán before the end of the month, as well as his wives, children and court. At the beginning of the following month the Maghrabin was conducted to the idol-temple; but the demon came not, and the Berber recited the Kurán till the morning, when the Sultan and his subjects arrived and found him so employed. Then they broke the idols, and razed the temple to the ground. The people of the island embraced Islám, and sent messengers to the other islands, whose inhabitants were also converted. The Maghrabin remained among them, and enjoyed their high esteem. The natives made profession of his doctrine, which was that of the *Imân Mâlic.* Even at present they respect the Maghrabins for his sake. He built a mosque, which is known by his name. I have also read the following inscription graven in wood on the enclosed pulpit of the

---

* *Chénoûrâzah*:—Cf. S. *Senarat* 'King (Chief Commander) of the army' and *Seneviratna* 'the gem-like General.'—*B.*

grand mosque: "*Sultan Ahmed Chénoûrâzah has received the true faith at the hands of Abou'lbérécât the Berber, the Maghrabin.*" This Sultan assigned a third of the taxes of the islands as alms to travelling foreigners in recognition of his reception of Islám through their agency. This share of the taxes still bears a name which recalls this event.

Owing to the demon in question many of the Máldive islands were depopulated before their conversion to Islám. When I reached the country I was not aware of this matter. One night, when I was at one of my occupations, I heard of a sudden people crying with loud voice the formulæ, "There is no God but God" and "God is very great." I saw children carrying Kuráns on their heads, and women rapping the insides of basins and vessels of copper. I was astonished at their conduct and said "What is happening"? and they replied "Do you not see the sea"? Upon which I looked and saw a kind of large ship, seemingly full of lamps and chafing-dishes. They said to me "that is the demon; he is wont to show himself once a month: but when once we have done as you have seen, he turns back and does us no harm.*

Of the Queen of these Islands.

One of the marvels of the Máldives is that they have for their Sovereign a woman, by name *Khadîdjah,* daughter of the Sultan *Djélâl eddîn 'Omar,* son of the Sultan *Salâh eddîn Sâlih Albendjâly.* The kingdom had at one time been possessed by her grandfather, then by her father, and when the latter died, her brother, *Chihâb eddîn,* became King. He was a minor, and the Vizier *'Abd Allah,* son of *Mohammed Alhadhramy*

---

* Vestiges of this romantic legend of their conversion to Muhammadanism live in the traditions of the Islanders to this day. But with more probability, they assign to a Shaikh *Yúsup Shams-ud-din* of *Tabrij* the honour, which Ibn Batúta not unnaturally would claim for a Maghrabin, and the votaries of Hazrat Mírá Sáhib for the Nágúr saint (C.A. S. Journ., No. 24, pp. 125–36 1881). Their first royal convert to Islám the Máldivians commonly know as "*Darumavanta* (= S. *Dharmmavanta,* i. e., 'the Just') *Rasgefánu.*" The mosque he built still stands, and continues to bear his name.—*B,*

espoused his mother and assumed authority over him. He is the same personage who married the Sultana *Khadîdjah* after the death of her first husband, the Vizier *Djèmâl eddîn*, as we shall describe hereafter. When *Chihâb eddîn* attained full age he ousted his step-father *'Abd Allah* and banished him to the islands of *Souweïd.* He was then left in sole possession, and chose as Vizier one of his freedmen by name *'Aly Calaky,** whom he deposed at the end of three years and banished to *Souweïd.* It is related of the Sultan *Chihâb eddîn* that he consorted nightly with the wives of the public officers and with courtezans. On that account he was deposed and deported to the province of *Hélédouteny (above spelt* Hélédommety): afterwards some one was sent and put him to death.

There then remained of the royal family only the sisters of the deceased, *Kadîdjah* who was the eldest, *Miryam* and *Fathimah.* The natives raised *Kadîdjah* to the throne, who was married to their preacher *Djémâl eddîn.* The latter became Vizier and master of the situation† and promoted his son *Mohammed* to the office of Preacher in his own stead: but orders were promulgated only in the name of *Khadîdjah.* These are traced on palm leaves by means of an iron [style] bent down resembling a knife. They write on paper only the Kuráns and scientific treatises. The Preacher makes mention of the Sultana on Fridays and on other days [of public prayer]; and here are the terms used, "O God, succour Thy servant, whom Thou hast in Thy wisdom preferred before other mortals, and whom Thou hast made the instrument of Thy mercy towards all Musalmáns, namely, the Sultana *Khadîdjah* daughter of Sultan *Djélâl eddîn*, son of Sultan *Salâh eddîn*." |

When a stranger comes among these people and repairs to the hall of audience, which is called *dâr*,‡ custom requires that he

* *'Aly Calaky*:—i.e., *'Alí Kalége.* The title *Kalége-fánu* or *Kalóge-fánu* (Pyrard, *Callogue*) accrues by purchase, not by birth.—*B.*

† *Mâitre de l'autorité*:—Major A. Ewing suggests "head of affairs" (Ar, *'ralba' 'al ellamar*).—*B.*

‡ *Dâr*:—Ar. 'house.'—*B.*

should take with him two cloths. He makes obeisance before the Sultana and throws down one of these cloths. Then he salutes her Vizier, who is also her husband, *Djémal eddîn*, and throws down the other. The army of this Queen consists of about a thousand men of foreign birth; some of the soldiers are natives. They come every day to the hall of audience to salute her and then go home. Their pay is in rice, supplied to them at the *bender* (*v. s.*, p. 10) every month. When the month is ended, they present themselves at the audience hall, and, saluting the Vizier, say, "Convey our respects (*to the Queen*) and inform her that we have come to request our pay." Thereupon the necessary orders are given in their favour. The Kází and ministers, who have with the people the title of Viziers, also present themselves every day at the audience hall. They make a salutation, and go away after the eunuchs have transmitted their respects to the Queen.

OF THE MINISTERS AND THEIR CONDUCT OF GOVERNMENT.

The people of the Máldives call the Grand Vizier, the Sultana's Lieutenant; *Calaky**; and the Kází *Fandayarkâloû.*† All judgments are in the jurisdiction of the Kází: he is more highly esteemed by the people than all other men, and his orders are executed as well as those of the Sultan and even better. He sits upon a carpet in the audience hall: he possesses three islands‡, whose revenue he places to his private account, after an ancient custom

* *Calaky*:—? Pers. Pyrard has *Quilague* "regent elect for the kingdom to act in absence of the Sultan" (Gray). [The title *Kilage-fánu* is not restricted to one grandee in the realm. At least three living Máldivian nobles have a right to the designation.—*B.*]

† *Fandayarkâloû*:—i. e. *Fadiyáru Kalóge-fánu* (Pyrard, *Pandiare*; Chris. *Fandiarhee*) the Chief Priest or Kází. Cf: T. *Pándiya.—B.*

‡ Corresponding with *nindagam* lands in Ceylon, the tenure of which is thus explained in Sir J. D'Oyley's M.S. "Constitution of the Kandyan Kingdom," a copy of which is in my possession :—'*Nindagama.*—A village which, for the time being, is the entire property of the grantee, or temporary chief; definitely granted by the king with *sannas*, it becomes *paraveny*, &c.,' p. 144. A '*gallat gama*' in the lower part of the Four Kóralés, Three Kóralés, and in parts of Sabaragamuwa is a similar tenure.

established by the Sultan *Áhmed Chénoûrâzah.* The Preacher is called *Hendîdjéry**: the Chief of the Treasury, *Fâmeldâry*†: the Receiver General of Revenue, *Mâfâcaloû*‡: the Minister of Police, *Fitnâyec*§: and the admiral, *Mânâyec*§. All these have the title of Vizier. There is no prison in these islands: criminals are shut up in wooden houses built to contain the merchants' goods. Each one is placed in a wooden cell, as we have (*in Morocco*) for the Christian prisoners.

OF MY ARRIVAL AT THESE ISLANDS AND OF THE VICISSITUDES WHICH I EXPERIENCED THERE.

When I came to this country I landed at *Cannaloûs* ‖, an island fair to behold, where there are many mosques. I was lodged

---

* *Hendîdjéry*:—i. e., *Hadégiri*, also known as *Boḍu Baḍéri*, in whom are combined now-a-days the offices of Chief of the Treasury and Receiver-General of Revenue. Pyrard writes *Endequery*, "a lord privy councillor, always in attendance upon the King"; Chris. *Hindegeree* 'Treasurer' (Gray). Cf: the *Bhánḍágáriko amachcho* (Turnour's Maháwaŋso, p. 231, 3) of the old Siŋhalese court.—*B.*

† *Fâmeldâry*:—i. e., *Fámuḍéri* (*Kilage-fánu*). Pyrard calls one of the great lords *Pammedery çalogue*, and Christopher says the 4th Vizier was styled *Famederi*, but had no distinct duties assigned him. Cf: *S. pámok, deḷa* and Maháwaŋso, p. 69, *amachcha pámukha.*—*B.*

‡ *Mâfâcaloû*:—i. e., *Mafaï* (*Kalóge-fánu*). According to Pyrard the *Manpas* (a probable misprint for *Maupas*) was "chancellor, keeper of the king's privy seal" (Gray). Chris. calls this officer *Mafae*, 5th Vizier. Cf: *S. Mahá* and *pati* in *senápati, chamúpati* (Maáhv. *passim*).—*B.*

§ *Fitnâyec*; *Mânâyec*:—These titles have not survived. Cf: S. *Mahá, náyaka.* Pyrard styles the "First Lord of the Admiralty and President of Board of Trade" (Gray) *Velannas* [*Velánâ*], and Chris. *Wilono Shadander*, 3rd Vizier. Ibn Batútá makes no mention of the *Dorhiméná* and *Hakurá* (Chris. *Durimind*: *Hakura*) 1st and 2nd Viziers; Pyrard, *Dorimenaz, Torimesnas*, "commander in chief of the army"; *Acouraz*). For particulars regarding the present government officers at Málé, see Ceylon Sess. Papers, 1881, "The Máldive Islands."—*B.*

‖ *Cannaloûs*:—As Ibn Batúta here mentions an island of the same name above given to one of the "zones" or atolls, the French editors are likely in error in identifying it with Collomandu atoll, there being no island in that

at the house of one of the most pious inhabitants. The lawyer *'Aly* gave me a feast. He was a distinguished person and had sons addicted to study I saw there a man named *Mohammed* a native of *Zhafâr Alhomoûdh,* who entertained me and said to me, "If you set foot on the island of *Mahal,* the Vizier will forcibly detain you, for the people have no Kází." It was then my intention to get away from that country to Ma'bar (*Coromandel coast*), to Serendîb (*Ceylon*), to Bengal, and then to China. I had then arrived at the Máldives in a ship whose captain was *'Omar Alhinaoury,* who was one of the virtuous pilgrims. When we had come into harbour at *Cannaloûs,* he remained there ten days: then he hired a little barque to take him thence to *Mahal,* bearing a present for the Queen and her Consort. I wished to go with him, but he said, "The barque is not big enough for you and your companions: if you like to set out without them, it is your affair." I declined this proposal, and *'Omar* took his departure. But the wind was contrary (*literally 'played with him'*) and at the end of four days he came back to us, not without having experienced trouble. He made his excuses to me, and implored me to go with him, my companions and all. We set sail in the morning and towards midday disembarked on an island: leaving that, we passed the night at another. After a four days cruise, we arrived at the province of *Teïm,* the governor of which was one *Hilâl.* He welcomed me, and gave me a feast: and afterwards came to visit me accompanied by four men, two of whom had on their shoulders a rod* from which were suspended four chickens. The other two had a similar rod to which were attached about ten coconuts. I was

atoll of the name Cannaloûs or one resembling it. It is unlikely too that Ibn Batúta coming from the north made his landing at a point so far south as Ҫollomandu. The termination '*lous,*' moreover or '*lu*' seems in the modern names of the islands to be quite distinct from '*du.*' [*V. s.*, p. 5, for identification of this island with *Kinaḷos* in Máḷosmaḍulu Atol. M. *ḷos* = ? the *bois mapou* tree of the Chagos group : M. *dú* = S. *díva* 'islet.'—*B.*]

* M. *dadimáru*—the *katliya* of the Siṇhalese—*B.*

surprised that they thought so highly of these common objects: but was informed that they do this as a token of consideration and respect.*

After leaving these people we landed on the sixth day at the island of *Othmân*, a distinguished man and one of the best one could meet. He received us with honour and entertained us. On the eighth day we put into an island belonging to a Vizier named *Télemdy*. On the tenth, we at length reached the island of *Mahal*, where the Sultana and her Consort reside, and cast anchor in the harbour. It is a custom of the country that no one may disembark without the permission of the inhabitants.† This was accorded to us: and I then desired to betake myself to some mosque, but the slaves on the beach prevented me, saying, "It is necessary that you should first visit the Vizier." I had requested the captain when he should be questioned about me to say, "I know nothing of him"; for fear lest they should detain me, being unaware that some ill-advised babbler had written to them an account of me, and that I had been Kází at Delhi. On our arrival at the audience hall, we took our seats on benches at the third entrance door. The Kází *'Içа Alyamany* came up and welcomed me, while I saluted the Vizier. The ship captain *Ibrâhîm* (*above he is called* 'Omar) brought ten pieces of worked stuffs, made a salute before the Queen, and threw down one of them: then he bent the knee in honor of the Vizier and threw down another, and so on to the last. He was questioned about me, and replied, "I know nothing of him."

We were then presented with betel and rose-water which is a mark of honor with them. The Vizier gave us lodging in a house and sent us a repast consisting of a large bowl full of rice and surrounded with plates of salted meats dried in the sun, chickens, melted butter and fish. On the morrow I set out with the captain and the Kází, *'Içа Alyamany* to visit a hermitage

* The Siṇhalese *penumkaḍa* or pingo of presents of sweetmeats, provisions, fruits, &c.

† Enforced to this day—*B*,

situated at the extremity of the island and founded by the virtuous Shaikh *Nedjîb.** We returned at night, and on the following morning the Vizier sent me some raiment, and a repast comprising rice, melted butter, salt, sun-dried meat, coconuts, and honey extracted from the same fruit, called by the natives *korbâny*,† signifying 'sugar-water.' They brought me also 100,000 cowries for my expenses. After ten days there arrived a ship from Ceylon, having on board some Persian and Arab fakírs who knew me and told the servants of the Vizier all about me. This enhanced the pleasure given by my coming. He sent for me at the commencement of Ramazán. I found the Chiefs and Viziers already assembled: food was served at the tables, each of which accommodated a certain number of guests. The Grand Vizier made me sit by his side, in company of the Kází *'Iça*, the *Fâmeldâry* Vizier or Chief of the Treasury, and the Vizier *'Omar*, the *Déherd*,‡ *i. e.*, General of the army. The dinner of these islanders consists of rice, chickens, melted butter, fish, salt, sun-dried meat, and cooked bananas. After eating, they drink the coco honey mingled with aromatics, which facilitates digestion.

On the 9th of Ramazán, the son-in-law of the Vizier died. His wife, the daughter of that minister, had already been married to the Sultan *Chihâb eddîn:* but neither of her husbands had cohabited with her on account of her youth. Her father, the

* This old shrine *(Najibu miskitu)*, it is said, may still be seen at Málé.—*B.*

† *Korbâny:*—Probably ought to be '*hakorbany*' equivalent to the Siŋhalese *hakuru*, 'jaggery': *peni*, 'honey,' the former word appearing as *acourou* for 'coco-honey' in the vocabulary of Pyrard.

‡ *Déherd:*—Cf. Pyrard, *Darade Tacourou* "count or duke," and Chris. *Dahara*, 6th Vizier. "As each incumbent of the first five Vizierships died no successor appears to have been appointed, and the titles thus gradually became extinct. That of the 6th Vizier alone survives in the person of the son of the former *Dáhará*......The *Dáhará (Takuru-fánu)* has no specific department of public business to supervise. But for a certain voice in military and municipal affairs his office would be a titular sinecure." (*The Máldive Islands*, Ceylon Sess. Pap. 1881). Cf: the Siŋhalese *Dovárika* (Maháv. p. 117, 11), but also the Persian *Daroogha.*—*B.*

Vizier, took her back home, and gave me her house, which was one of the most charming. I asked permission to entertain the fakírs returning from visiting the Foot of Adam, in the island of Ceylon (*see below*). This he granted, and sent me five sheep, a rare animal with the islanders, having to be brought from Ma'bar (*Coromandel Coast*) from Malabar and from *Makdachaou*. The Vizier sent me also rice, chickens, melted butter and spices. I had all these carried to the house of the Vizier *Souleïmân*, the *Mânâyec* (*Admiral*), who took the greatest care in having them cooked, augmented them in quantity, and sent me carpets and copper vessels. We broke the fast according to custom, in the palace of the Sultana, with the Grand Vizier, and I requested him to permit some of the other Viziers to assist at my dinner. He said "I will come myself too." I thanked him and returned home: but he had already arrived with the Viziers and grandees of the State. He seated himself in a raised pavilion of wood. All who came, whether Chiefs or Viziers, saluted the Grand Vizier, and threw down a piece of unworked stuff, in such numbers that the total reached to a hundred or thereabouts, all of which the fakírs appropriated. Dinner was then served and eaten: then the readers of the Kurán gave a reading with their fine voices, after which were singing and dancing. I had a fire prepared, and the fakírs then entered and trampled it under foot; some of them even ate the live embers, as one would devour sweetmeats, until the flame was extinguished.

The Story of some of the Vizier's benefactions to me.

When the night was ended, the Vizier went home and I accompanied him. We passed a garden belonging to the Treasury, and the Vizier said to me, "This garden is for you: I will have a house built upon it to serve for your residence." I praised his kind action, and made vows in his favour. Next day he sent me a young female slave, and his messenger said, "The Vizier bids me say, if this girl pleases you, she is yours: otherwise he will send a Mahratta slave." I liked the young Mahratta girls, so I replied "I desire only the Mahratta," The minister had one brought to me, by name *Gulistán*, which signifies "the flower of the garden" *(or more exactly 'the parterre of flowers')*. She knew the Persian tongue, and pleased me highly. The Máldive inhabitants have a language which I did not understand.

The next day, the Vizier sent me a young female slave from Coromandel by name *Anbéry* (*ambergris colour*). On the following evening he came to my house with some of his servants, and entered attended by two little [boy] slaves. I saluted him, and he asked me how I did. I made vows for his welfare and thanked him. One of the slaves put before him a *lokchah* (*bokchah*),* that is, a kind of napkin, from which he drew some silk stuffs and a box containing pearls and trinkets. The Vizier made me a present of them, adding, "If I had sent these with the young slave, she would have said 'This is my property: I brought it from the house of my master.' Now that the things belong to you, make her a present of them." I addressed prayers to God for the minister, and rendered to him expressions of my gratitude, of which he was worthy.

Of the Vizier's change of disposition towards me of the project which I formed to depart; and of my continued sojourn at the Máldives.

The Vizier *Souleïmân*, the *Mânâyec*, had proposed to me to espouse his daughter. I sent to ask the permission of the Vizier *Djémâl eddîn* to conclude the marriage. My messenger returned saying, "It does not please him; he wishes you to marry his daughter when the legal term of her widowhood shall have expired." I refused to consent to this union, fearing the sinister fortune attached to the daughter of the Vizier, since two husbands had already died without having consummated the marriage. In the midst of all this a fever seized me, and I was very ill.

* *Lokchah* or *bokchah*:—If the latter be the correct reading = ? *burugá* the cloth worn over the face at times by Máldive ladies.—*B.*

Every person who goes to that island must inevitably catch the fever.* I made a strong resolve to get out of the country: I sold a portion of my trinkets for cowries, and chartered a ship to take me to Bengal. When I went to take my leave of the Vizier, the Kází coming out met me, and addressed me in these terms, "The Vizier," said he, "bids me tell you this 'If you wish to go away, give us back what we have given you and then go.'" I replied, "With a part of my trinkets I have bought cowries; do with them what you will." In a little while the Kází returned to me and said, "The Vizier says 'We have given you gold, not cowries,'" I replied, "Very well: I will sell them and will pay you gold." Accordingly I sent to request the merchants to buy the shells from me. But the Vizier gave them orders not to deal with me; for his design, in so conducting himself, was to prevent me going away from him.

Then he deputed one of his intimates, who had this conversation with me, "The Vizier bids me request you to remain with us and you shall have everything you desire." So I said to myself, "I am under their authority: if I do not stay with a good grace, I shall have to stay by constraint: a voluntary sojourn is preferable to that." I therefore made reply to the envoy, "Very well: I shall remain with him." The messenger returned to his master, who was delighted with my reply, and sent for me. When I entered his presence, he got up and embraced me, saying, "We wish you to remain with us, and you wish to go!" I made my excuses, which were accepted, and said, "If you wish me to stay, I will impose upon you certain conditions." The Vizier replied, "We accept them: please to name them." I answered, "I am unable to walk on foot." For it is a custom of the country that

* "On la connoist par toute l' Inde sous le nom de fiévre des Maldives. Ils l'appellent *Malé ons* [*hun* or *huma*]. C'est de cette maladie que la pluspart de mes compagnons estoient morts, comme tous estrangers ne manquent pas d'en estre bientost atteints," (Pyrard, p. 95; again p. 201). The Indian Navy Surveyors (1834–6) suffered much from this pest of the group.—*B.*

no one rides on horseback, except the Vizier. So it was that when I had a horse* given to me and was mounted, the crowd of men, as well as children, began to follow me with astonishment, whereof I complained to the Vizier. Accordingly a *donkorah* was beaten, and it was proclaimed among the people that no one should follow me. The *donkorah* is a kind of copper basin, which is struck with an iron rod [or hammer], and gives a noise heard afar.† After it is struck, the crier cries in public whatever he required.

The Vizier said to me, "If you wish to ride in a palaquin, well and good: otherwise we have a stallion and a mare: choose which of these animals you prefer." I chose the mare which was brought to me at once. At the same time some garments were brought to me. I said to the Vizier, "What shall I do with the cowries which I have bought?" He replied, "Send one of your companions to sell them for you in Bengal." "I will do so," said I, "on condition that you send some one to help him in the affair." "I will," he replied. So I despatched my comrade *Abou Mohammed,* son of *Ferhân,* in whose company they sent one called the pilgrim *'Aly.* But it happened that a storm arose: the crew jettisoned the whole cargo, including even the mast, the water, and all the other provisions for the voyage. They remained for sixteen days without sail, rudder, &c.; and after the endurance of hunger, thirst, and toil, they arrived at the island of Ceylon. In a year's time my comrade *Abou Mohammed* came back to me. He had visited the Foot *(of Adam)* and he afterwards saw it again with me.

Account of the Festival in which I took part with the Islanders.

The month of Ramazán ended, the Vizier sent me some [proper] raiment, and we made our way to the place consecrated

---

* In November, 1879, there were but two horses in the Islands, the property of the Sultan at Málé, "wretched wry-legged weeds, not fit to ride," and kept merely for show.—*B.*

† *Donkorah:*—Ibn Batúta's ignorance of the Máldive language may possibly have led him to confuse *dummárhi,* the term for the 'flagiolet,' with *koli* 'gong.' The iron striker is called *daḍigaḍu.*—*B.*

for prayer. The path which the minister had to traverse, between his residence and the place of prayer, had been decorated: stuffs had been spread, and there had been placed to right and left heaps (*literally* cotta's, *v. s.*, *p.* 11) of cowries. All the Emirs and grandees who had houses on the road had planted near them little coco-trees, arecas, and bananas. Ropes were hung from one tree to the next, and green nuts were suspended from the ropes. The master of the house remained near the gate, and when the Vizier passed, he threw before his feet a piece of silk or cotton. The slaves of the minister appropriated these, as well as the cowries placed by the way. The Vizier advanced on foot, covered with an ample robe of goat's hair of Egyptian manufacture, and with a large turban. As a scarf he wore a kerchief of silk; four umbrellas shaded his head, and sandals covered his feet. All his attendants without exception had their feet bare. Trumpets, clarions, and drums* preceded him: the soldiers marched before and behind him, all shouting the cry "*God is very great!*" until they were arrived at the place of prayer.

Prayer ended, the son of the Vizier preached: then was brought a litter which the Vizier mounted. The Emirs and the other grandees again saluted him, casting down pieces of stuffs according to custom. Before this time the Grand Vizier used not to ride in a litter, for the Kings alone did so. The bearers then lifted it; I mounted my horse, and we entered the palace. The minister seated himself at a raised dais, having near him the Viziers and the Emirs. The slaves remained standing, bearing shields, swords, and staves.† Food was then served, and afterwards arecanuts and betel, after which was brought a little dish containing sandal *mokassiry*.‡ As soon as one party of the guests

---

* M. *tálafili*; *dummárhi*; *beru.*—*B.*

† M *aḍḍana*; *kaḍi*; *daḍi.*—*B.*

‡ *Mokassury*: = ? M. *kasturi* '*musk.*'—*B.*

had eaten, they rubbed themselves with sandal. That day I saw upon one of their dishes a fish of the species of sardines, salted and raw, which had been sent as a present from *Caoulem*. This fish is very abundant on the Malabar Coast. The Vizier took a sardine, and began to eat it, at the same time saying to me, "Eat some of that; it is not found in our country." I answered, "How can I eat it? It is not cooked." "It is cooked," said he. But I replied, "I know this fish well, for it abounds in my native land."

OF MY MARRIAGE AND OF MY NOMINATION TO THE DIGNITY OF KÁZI.

On the 10th day of Shawwál I agreed with the Vizier *Souleïmân Mânâyec*, or Admiral, that I should espouse his daughter, and I sent to request the Vizier *Djémâl eddîn* that the betrothal should take place in his presence at the palace. He agreed and sent betel, according to custom, and sandal. The people were present for the ceremony. The Vizier *Souleïmân* delayed his coming. He was sent for: and yet he came not. He was sent for a second time, and he excused himself on account of the illness of his daughter: but the Grand Vizier said to me in private, "His daughter refuses to marry; and she is mistress of her own actions. But see! the people are assembled: would you like to espouse the step-mother of the Sultana, the widow of her father?" (The Grand Vizier's son was then married to this woman's daughter). I replied "Yes, by all means." He then convoked the Kází and the notaries. The profession of the Musalmán faith was then recited, and the Vizier paid the dowry. After some days my wife was brought to me. She was one of the best women who ever lived. Such was her good manners, that when I became her husband, she anointed me with scented oils and perfumed my clothes; during this operation she laughed and allowed nothing disagreeable to be seen.

When I had married this lady, the Vizier constrained me to accept the functions of the Kází. The cause of my nomination was that I had reproached the Kází for taking the tenth part of inheritances, when he made partition among the heirs. I said to him, "You ought to have only a fee, which you should agree for with the heirs." This judge did nothing rightly. After I was invested with the dignity of Kází, I used all my efforts to have the precepts of the law observed. Disputes are not settled in that country as in ours. The first bad custom which I reformed concerned the sojourn of divorced women at the houses of those who had repudiated them; for these women did not cease to remain at the houses of their former husbands, until they got married to others. I prevented this being done under any pretext. About five and twenty men were brought to me who had conducted themselves in this sort. I had them beaten with whips,* and had them marched through the bazárs. As for the women, I compelled them to leave the homes of these men. Next I exerted myself to get prayers celebrated: I ordered some men to run down the streets and bazárs immediately after the Friday's prayers. If any were discovered, who had not prayed, I had him beaten and marched through the town. I compelled the *Imâms* and *Mouezzins* in possession of fixed appointments to apply themselves assiduously in their duties. I wrote in the same sense to *(the magistrates of)* all the other islands. Lastly I essayed to make the women dress themselves, but in this I did not succeed.

OF THE ARRIVAL OF THE VIZIER *'ABD ALLAH*, SON OF *MOHAMMED ALHADHRAMY* WHOM SULTAN *CHIHAB EDDIN* HAD BANISHED TO *SOUWEID*: ACCOUNT OF WHAT PASSED BETWEEN US.

I had espoused the step-daughter of this personage, and I loved this wife very dearly. When the Grand Vizier recalled him to the Island of *Mahal*, I sent him presents, went to meet

* M. *durrá*. Pyrard has *gleau* "leathern thongs used for corporal punishment."—*B*.

him, and accompanied him to the palace. He saluted the Grand Vizier, who lodged him in a magnificent house, and there I often visited him. It happened, when I passed the month of Ramazán in prayer, that all the inhabitants visited me, except *'Abd-Allah*. The Vizier *Djémâl eddîn* himself came to see me, and *'Abd-Allah* with him, but only bearing him company. Enmity arose between us. Afterwards when I came out of my retreat, the maternal uncles of my wife, the step-daughter of *'Abd-Allah* made a complaint to me. They were the sons of the Vizier *Djémâl eddîn Assindjary*. Their father had appointed the Vizier *'Abd-Allah* to be their guardian, and their property was still in his hands, although they had by the law emerged from wardship. They demanded his appearance in Court. It was my custom when I summoned one of the contending parties to send him a slip of paper, either with or without writing. On delivery of that the party repaired to the Court; if he did not, I punished him. In this way I sent a slip to *'Abd-Allah*. This procedure raised his choler, and on account thereof he conceived a hatred for me. He concealed his enmity and sent some one to plead for him. Some unseemly language was reported to me as having been used by him.

The islanders, both gentle and simple, were accustomed to salute the Vizier *'Abd-Allah* in the same way as the Vizier *Djémâl eddîn*. Their salutation consists in touching the ground with the forefinger, then kissing it, and placing it on the head. I issued orders to the public crier, and he proclaimed in the Queen's palace in the presence of witnesses, that whoever should render homage to *'Abd-Allah* in like manner as to the Grand Vizier should incur severe chastisement. And I exacted from him a promise that he would not allow men to do so. His enmity against me was now increased. Meantime I married another wife, daughter of a highly esteemed Vizier, whose grandfather was the Sultan *Dâovd*, the grand-son of the Sultan

*Ahmed Chénoûrâzah.** Then I married one who had been married to the Sultan *Chihâb eddîn*, and I had three houses built in the garden which the Vizier gave to me. My fourth wife, the step-daughter of *'Abd-Allah*, lived at her own house. She was the one of all my wives whom I cherished the most. Thus allied by marriage to the persons named, the Vizier and the people of the island feared me much, by reason of their own weakness. False reports were spread between me and the Grand Vizier, in great part by the care of the Vizier *'Abd-Allah*, so that our estrangement became final.

Of my departure from these people, and of the motive thereof.

It happened that one day the wife of a slave of the late Sultan *Djelâl eddîn* made a complaint of him to the Vizier, to the effect that he had a liaison with one of the Sultan's concubines. The Vizier sent witnesses, who entered the girl's house and found the slave asleep with her upon the same carpet. Both were taken into custody. In the morning, on being informed of this, I went to the audience hall and took my seat in my customary place. I made no reference to the affair. A courtier then approached me and said, "The Vizier requests to know if you have any business with him." I replied, "No." The design of the minister was that I should speak of the affair of the concubine and the slave; for it was my invariable rule to decide every case which he put before me. But as I was showing him my dissatisfaction and dislike, I omitted to do so then. I went straightway to my own house and took my seat where I delivered my judgments. Soon after came a Vizier, saying on behalf of the Grand Vizier, "Yesterday, so and so occurred in

---

* This relationship fixes approximately the date of *Chénoûrâzah* and of the Muhammedan conversion, which may have been as early as 1200 A. D., but--allowing for early marriages—perhaps more probably about 1220, or 1230 A.D.—See Paper on the Maldives, J. R. A. S., Vol. X., N., S., 1878., p. 177.

the matter of the concubine and slave : judge both of them conformably with the law." I replied, " It is a cause in which it is not fitting to deliver judgment save at the Sultan's palace." I then returned thither : the people assembled, and the concubine and the slave were summoned. I ordered that both should be beaten for their liaison ; and adjudged that the woman should be set at liberty and the slave kept in prison : after which I returned home.

The Vizier sent several of his principal attendants to speak to me about setting the slave at liberty. I said to them, " Intercession is made with me in favor of a negro slave, who has violated the respect which he owed to his master; while but yesterday, you have deposed the Sultan *Chihâb eddîn* and slain him, because he went into the house of one of his slaves." Thereupon I ordered the prisoner to be beaten with bambu switches, which produced more effect than the whip. I had him marched through the whole island, with a rope round his neck. The messengers of the Vizier went and informed him of what passed. He discovered great agitation and was inflamed with anger. He assembled the other Viziers, the chiefs of the army, and sent for me. I obeyed the summons. It was my custom to pay him homage by bending the knee. This time I did not do so, only saying "Peace be with you !" * Then I said to those present, " Be ye witnesses that I resign my functions as Kází, because I am rendered powerless to exercise them." The Vizier having then bespoke me, I went up and took a seat in front of him, and then I answered him in terms yet more severe. After this rencontre, the *Mouezzin* made the call to prayer at sun-down, and the Grand Vizier entered his house, saying, " It is pretended that I am a sovereign; but see ! I have sent for this man in order to vent my wrath upon him, and he dares to be angry with me." I was only respected by these islanders for the sake of the Sultan of India, for they knew the position I occupied under

* *Salaam alescon !*—Ar.

him. Although they are far removed from him, they fear him much in their hearts.

When the Grand Vizier had returned to his house, he sent the deposed Kází, an eloquent speaker, who addressed me as follows:—"Our master requires to know why you have violated, in the presence of witnesses, the respect which is due to him, and why you have not rendered him homage?" I replied, "I saluted him only when my heart was satisfied with him; but now that dissatisfaction has supervened, I have renounced the usage. The salutation of Musalmans consists only of the word *assèlâm*, (*Peace be with you!*) and that I have pronounced." The Vizier sent this person a second time, and he then said, "You have no other aim but that of leaving us; pay the dowries of your wives, and what you owe to the men, and go when you will." At this speech I bowed and went to my house and paid such debts as I had contracted. Up to this time the Vizier had given me carpets and a suite of furniture, consisting of copper vessels, and other things. He used to grant me everything I asked; he loved me and treated me with consideration; but his disposition changed and he became inspired with fear of me.

When he heard that I had paid my debts and that I was intending to depart, he repented of what he had said, and put off granting me permission to go. I adjured him by the strongest oaths that I was under necessity to resume my voyage. I removed my belongings to a mosque upon the beach, and repudiated one of my wives. Another was with child, to her I gave a term of nine months, within which I might return, or in default thereof she was to be mistress of her own actions. I took with me that one of my wives who had been married to the Sultan *Chihâb eddîn* in order to restore her to her father who dwelt in the island of *Moloûc*, and my first wife, whose daughter was half-sister to the Sultana. I agreed with the Vizier *'Omar Dehcrd* (*or General of the army, v. s. p.* 22) and the Vizier

Haçan, the Admiral, that I should go to the country of *Ma'bar** (*Coromandel*), the king of which was my brother-in-law, and that I should return with troops, to the end that the islands might be reduced under his authority, and that I should then exercise the power in his name. I chose to serve as signals between us, white flags to be hoisted on board the vessels. As soon as they should see these, they were to rise in rebellion on shore. I never had any such idea, up to the day when I showed my displeasure. The Vizier was afraid of me and said to the people, "This man is determined to get the Vizierate, me living or dead." He made many enquiries about me, and added, "I have heard that the King of India has sent him money, to use in raising trouble against me." He dreaded my departure lest I should return from the Coromandel Coast with troops. He bade me remain until he should get a ship ready for me: but I refused.

The half-sister of the Queen complained to her of the departure of her mother with me. The Queen wished to prevent her, but did not succeed. When she saw her resolved to go, she said to her, "All the trinkets you possess were provided with money from the custom-house. If you have witnesses to swear that *Djélâl eddîn* gave them to you, good and well; otherwise restore them." These trinkets were of considerable value; nevertheless my wife gave them up to these people. The Viziers and Chiefs came to me while I was at the mosque, and prayed me to return. I replied to them, "Had I not sworn, assuredly I would return." They said, "Go then to some other island, so that your oath be kept, and then return." "Very well," said I, to satisfy them. When the day of my departure

---

* The name *Ma'bar* ('passage' or 'ferry') was given to the Coromandel coast by the Arabs during the 13th and 14th centuries. Col. Yule suggests that it referred to the communication with Ceylon, or, as is more probable, to its being at that age the coast most frequented by travellers from Arabia and the Gulf (Marco Polo II., p. 268). The tract of coast called *Ma'bar* extended from Cape Comorin to Nellore.

was come, I went to bid adieu to the Vizier. He embraced me and wept in such wise that his tears fell upon my feet. He passed the following night watching in the island, for fear lest my connections by marriage and my comrades should rise in rebellion against him.

At length I got away and arrived at the island of the Vizier *'Aly*. My wife was in great distress, and wished to return. I repudiated her and left her there, and wrote this news to the Vizier, for she was the mother of his son's wife. I repudiated also the wife to whom I had fixed the term (*for my return*) and sent for a slave girl I was fond of. Meanwhile we sailed through the midst of the islands, from one group to another.

Of Women who have only one Breast.

In one of the islands I saw a woman who had only one breast. She was mother of two daughters, of whom one resembled her exactly, and the other had two breasts, only that one was large and full of milk, the other small and contained none. I was astonished at the conformation of these women.

We arrived in course at another of these islands which was small, and had a solitary house, occupied by a weaver,* a married man and father of a family. He possessed small coco trees, and a little barque,† which served him for fishing and visiting the other islands when he wished: on his islet were also small bananas trees. We saw there none of the birds of the continent, except two crows, which flew in front of us on our arrival and circled round our ship. I truly envied the lot of this man, and made a vow that if his island should belong to me, I would retire to it until the inevitable term should arrive for me.

---

* Mats, and some cloths, are woven in Huvadú (Suvádive) Atol; the former on the islands *Gaddú*, *Havara Tinadú*, and *Gemaná-furhi*.—*B.*

† M. *mas oḍi*.—*B.*

I next arrived at the island of *Moloûc,** where I found the ship belonging to the captain *Ibrâhîm* in which I had resolved to sail to the Coromandel Coast That person came to visit me along with his companions, and they entertained me at a fine feast. The Vizier had written in my favor an order requiring them to give me at this island 120 *bostoû* (*v. s. p.* 11) of cowries, 20 goblets of *athouân*† or coco-honey, and to add to that every day a certain quantity of betel, arecanuts, and fish. I remained at *Moloûc* 70 days, and married two wives there. *Moloûc* is one of the fairest islands to see, being verdant and fertile. Among other marvellous things to be seen there, I remarked that a branch cut off one of the trees there, and planted in the ground or on a wall, will cover itself with leaves and become itself a tree. I observed also that the pomegranate tree there ceases not to bear fruit the whole year round. The inhabitants of this island were afraid that the captain *Ibrâhîm* was going to harry them at his departure. They therefore wanted to seize the arms which his ship contained, and to keep them until the day of his departure. A dispute arose on this subject, and we returned to *Mahal,* but did not disembark. I wrote to the Vizier informing him of what had taken place. He sent a written order to the effect that there was no ground for seizing the arms of the crew. We then returned to *Moloûc,* and left it again in the middle of the month of Rabí the second of the year 745 (*26th August A. D. 1344*). In the month of Shabán of the same year (*December, 1344*), died the Vizier *Djémâl eddîn*. The Sultana was with child by him and was delivered after his death. The Vizier *'Abd-Allah* took her to wife.

---

* *Moloûc:*—Moluk, the chief island of Moluk Atol, is in lat. 2° 57′ N. The Admiralty Chart says that it possesses good water. [More probably *Fua Mulaku* Island, which lies detached a little S. E. of the centre of the Equatorial Channel (lat. 0° 17, S.) between Huvadú and Aḍḍú Atols. Ibn Batúta had already "sailed through the midst of the islands, from one group to another."—*B.*]

‡ *Athouân:*—Above at p. 22 coco-honey is called *korbâny*. In Moura's edition of Ibn Batúta (Lisbon, 1855), the word appears as *alatuan*.

As for us, we sailed on, though without an experienced pilot. The distance which separates the Máldives from the Coromandel Coast is three days' sail. We were for nine days under sail, and on the 9th we went on shore at the island of Ceylon. We perceived the mountain of *Sérendîb* raised in the air like a column of smoke. When we came near the island, the mariners said, "This port is not in the country of a Sultan in whose dominions the merchants can go in all safety; it is in the country of the Sultan *Aïry Chacarouaty** who is one of the unjust and perverse. He has ships engaged in piracy on the high seas." Wherefore we feared to land at his port, but, the wind rising, we were in danger of being swamped, and I said to the Captain, "Put me ashore and I will get for you a safe-conduct from this Sultan." He did as I requested, and put me out on the beach. The idolaters advanced to meet us and said, "Who are you?" I apprized them that I was the brother-in-law and friend of the Sultan of Coromandel, that I was on my way to pay him a visit, and that what was on board the ship was destined for a present to that prince. The natives went to their Sovereign and communicated to him my reply. He sent for me, and I presented myself before him at the town of *Batthâlah (Puttaḷam)*† which was his capitâl. It is

* *Aïry Chacarouaty:*—This seems to be the (?) Páṇḍiyan prince, "Aareya Chakkra Warti," mentioned in Pridham (Ceylon, Vol I.,p. 78), who, after 1371 A.D., conquered the northern half of the Island, and took King Wikrama captive, but was defeated by the Adigar Alakeswara, and possibly the same Malabar Prince captured and put to death by Prince "Sapoomal Cumara."—See Upham's Rájawali, p.264, 269. [A correspondent writes :—"The name identifies no individual. All the Kings of Jaffna seem to have been called Ariya or Ariyan—an old title in India. See the Khandagiri rock inscription, and one of those over the Manikpura cave at Udayagiri (Cunningham's Corpus Insc. Indic., Vol. I.) Jaffna at this period (A.D. 1344) was, if the *Vaipava Málai* can be trusted, under the rule of Kunavirasinka Ariyan."—*B.*]

† *Batthâlah:*—This town has been identified with Puttaḷam by Lee, Tennent, the French Editor, and Col. Yule, successively; but, it seems to me, without sufficient authority. The *â* of *Batthâlah* is against it; so too the want

a neat little place, surrounded by a wall and bastions of wood. All the neighbouring shore was covered with trunks of cinnamon trees, torn up by the torrents. This wood was collected on the beach, and formed as it were hillocks. The inhabitants of Coromandel and of Malabar take it away without payment, save only that in return for this favor they make a present to the Sultan of

---

of corroborative evidence of the existence of Puttaḷam as a town of any importance at this period, and the want of any river in its neighbourhood answering to the "torrents" spoken of by the traveller. This last point, and the doubtful existence of cinnamon so far north as Puttaḷam, are the only difficulties raised by Tennent (Vol. I., p. 580). The site of *Batthâlah* has to be found with a full consideration of the cinnamon question, and, of the site of *Mênâr Mendely*, the town at which Ibn Batúta: first halts on his journey towards the Peak. With his usual laborious care Tennent (Vol. I., p. 596) has examined all the early authorities known to him, and concludes that the text here gives the first mention of cinnamon as a product of Ceylon. Col. Yule, however (Marco Polo, Vol. II., p. 255), points out that two previous notices of it exist, one in Kazwini (*circa* A.D. 1275), the other in a letter from John of Montecorvino (*Ethe's Kazwini, 229; Cathay, 213.*)

The account given by our traveller shews that it was not as yet cultivated, and perhaps that the "trunks" seen by him were not those of the valuable variety of later days, but of the common indigenous *cassia*. I am not aware whether the cultivation, or growth, of cinnamon positively ceases at Chilaw, as seems to be the common opinion: but, even if this be true of the Ceylon cinnamon of commerce, it may not be so of the indigenous plant, and the area of production may be more limited now than in the 4th century. Ribeyro (Lee's edn., p. 15), says "there is a forest of it 12 leagues in extent between Chilaw and the pagoda of Tenevary," without saying that Chilaw is the northern limit: the French translator (at p. 11) in his note, remarks 'that it is only found between *Grudumalé* and *Tenevaré*.' Now the promontory of Kutiraimalai is a considerable distance north of Puttaḷam: and I have little doubt that the French translator had good authority for the assertion. The remaining difficulty, that of the "torrents," inclines me to believe that the site of *Batthâlah* was probably further north, near the mouth of the Kalá-oya, where the free access to the sea by the passage between Kalpiṭiya and Káratívu would seem to designate a more suitable situation for a Prince, whose strength lay in ships.

It now remains to fix *Mênâr Mendely*, which has been identified by preceding commentators, and not unnaturally, with the *Minneri Mundal* of

stuffs and such things. Between Coromandel and the island of Ceylon there is a distance of a day and a night. There is also found in this island plenty of brazil-wood,* as well as Indian aloes, called *alcalakhy* (*perhaps from the Greek* αγάλλοκον†), but which does not resemble the *kamâry* or the *kâkouly*.‡ We shall speak of them hereafter.

Of the Sultan of Ceylon.

He is called *Aïry Chacarouaty*, and he is a powerful King upon the sea. I saw in one day, while I was on the Coromandel

---

Arrowsmith's map, adopted by Tennent. This place is represented as upon the Calpentyn [Kalpiṭiya] peninsular, due west of Puttaḷam, and I could never account for the traveller taking it on his route to the Peak. I am now informed that no such place exists. There is, however, on the present road, about half way between Puttaḷam and Chilaw, a village called *Muntal* or *Mundal*, four miles north of the Battul-oya, which seems to me to suit the description of the traveller in every way. *Ménâr Mendely* was the frontier town of the *Batthâlah* Prince, as *Bender Sélâouât* (Chilaw) must (from the term *Bender*) have been to the Siṇhalese King of the South: and the low jungles of the neighbourhood have always been a favourite haunt of wild buffaloes. By the Census of 1871, I find Muṇdal and Táṇḍivila together had a population of 128, and Paniya Muntal, a neighbouring village, of 80. In conclusion, I have to state that the correspondent who has indicated the places on the Peak route, is of opinion that *Batthâlah* is Jaffna and *Ménâr Mendely*, Mannâr. I have been unable, after due consideration, to adopt his views, nor could I state them here at sufficient length. I trust, however, that if he has no objection he will formulate them in a separate paper for the use of the Society.

* *Brazil-wood*:—i.e., "sapan." "'They have brazil-wood, much the in the world.' Kazwini names it, and Ribeyro (Lee's edn., p. 16) does the like." —Yule, Marco Polo, Vol. II., pp. 254, 256.

† *Alcalakhy*:—Mr. L. Nell considers the surmise of the French editors correct. "Ibn Batúta evidently uses the Greek term *agallokon* corresponding to the Latin *Excaecaria agallocha*. The Socotrine variety of aloes is the usual medicinal species. Two indigenous species are known in India, the *Aloe Indica* and the *Aloe litoralis*. One of these grows freely in Puttaḷam, and is known by the Tamiḷ name, *takkali*."—*B*.

‡ *Kamâry; kâkouly*,—Dr. S. Lee (Travels of Ibn Batúta, p. 184) identifies the latter of these plants on the authority of Ibn Husain's Medical Dictionary.—*B*.

Coast, a hundred of his ships, both small and great, which had just arrived. There were in the port eight ships belonging to the Sultan of the country and destined to make the voyage to Yemen. The sovereign gave orders to make preparations, and assembled people to guard his vessels. When the Siṇhalese despaired of finding an opportunity of seizing them, they said, "We have only come to protect the vessels belonging to us, which also must go to Yemen."

When I entered the presence of the idolater Sultan, he rose, and made me sit by his side, and spoke to me with the greatest good-will. "Let your comrades," said he, "land in all safety, and be my guests until they leave. There is an alliance between me and the Sultan of Coromandel." Then he gave orders to have me lodged, and I remained with him for three days, in great consideration, which increased every day. He understood the Persian tongue, and much did he relish all I told him of foreign Kings and countries. I entered his presence one day when he had by him a quantity of pearls, which had been brought from the fishery in his dominions. The servants of the prince were sorting the precious from those which were not so. He said to me, "Have you seen the pearl fishery in the countries whence you have come?" "Yes," I answered, "I have seen it in the island of *Keïs*, and in that of *Kech*, which belong to *Ibn Assaoudmely*." "I have heard of them," replied he; and then took up some pearls and added, "Are there at that island any pearls equal to these?" I said, "I have seen none so good." My answer pleased him, and he said, "They are yours: do not blush," added he, "and ask of me anything you desire." I replied, "I have no other desire, since I have arrived in this island, but to visit the illustrious Foot of Adam." The people of the country call the first man *bâbâ* (*father*) and Eve, *mâmâ* (*mother*). "That is easy enough," answered he, "We shall send some one to conduct you." "That is what I wish," said I, and then added, "The vessel in which I have come will go in safety to *Ma'bar* and on my return, you will send me in your ships.' "By all means" said he.

When I reported this to the Captain of the ship, he said, "I will not go till you have returned, even though I should have to wait a year for you." I made known this answer to the Sultan, and he said, "The Captain shall be my guest until your return." He gave me a palanquin, which his slaves bore upon their backs, and sent with me four of those *djoguis* who are accustomed to undertake the pilgrimage annually to the Foot; he added to the party three Bráhmins, ten others of his friends, and fifteen men to carry the provisions. As for water, it is found in abundance on the route.

On the day of our departure, we encamped near a river, which we crossed in a ferry-boat formed of bamboos. Thence we took our way to *Ménâr Mendely*, a fine town, situated at the extremity of the Sultan's territory, the people of which treated us to an excellent repast. This consisted of young buffaloes, taken in chase in the neighbouring forest and brought in alive, rice, melted butter, fish, chickens and milk. We did not see in this town a single Musalmán, except a native of Khorassan, who had remained on account of sickness, and who now accompanied us. We left for *Bender Sélâouât,** a little town, and after quitting it we traversed some rough country, much of it under water. There were numbers of elephants there, which do no mann of harm to pilgrims, nor to strangers, and that is by the holy influence of Shaikh *Abou 'Abd Allah*, son of *Khafif*, the first who opened this way to visiting the Foot. Up to that time the infidels prevented the Musalmáns from accomplishing the pilgrimage,

---

* *Bender Sélâouât, i.e.*, Chilaw.—The fact that it was called *Bender*, implies, I think, that it contained a custom-house or store-house (*V. s.* p. 10), and was a frontier town of the King who ruled south of "Aareya Chakrawarti." This is confirmed by the description of *Ménâr Mendely* as the frontier town of "Aareya Chakrawarti."

harried them, and would not eat or deal with them. But when the adventure, which we have recounted in the first part of these Voyages (*Tome II, pp. 80, 81*) had happened to the Shaikh *Abou 'Abd Allah*, that is to say, the murder of all his companions by the elephants, his own preservation, and the manner in which the elephant carried him on its back, from that time on the idolaters have respected the Musalmans, have permitted them to enter their houses and to eat with them.* They also place confidence in them, as regards their women and children. Even to this day they venerate in the highest degree the above-named Shaikh, and call him 'the Great Shaikh.'

Meanwhile we reached the town of *Conacâr*,† the residence

* "In this statement Ibn Batúta is fully borne out by Robert Knox, who says, speaking of the charity of the Siṇhalese, in his Chapter 'concerning their religious doctrines, opinions, and practices,' Part iii., Ch. 5, 'Nor are they charitable only to the poor of their own nation; but, as I said, to others and particularly to the Moorish beggars, who are Mahometans by religion; these have a temple in Kandy. A certain former King gave this temple this privilege—that every freeholder should contribute a ponnam (fanam, 1½*d.*) to it; and these Moors go to every house in the land to receive it [except in Doḷosbágé]; and, if the house be shut, they have power to break it open, and take of goods to the value of it. They come very confidently when they beg, and say they come to fulfil the peoples' charity; and the people do liberally relieve them for charity's sake....... These Moors pilgrims have many pieces of land given to them by well disposed persons, out of charity, where they build houses and live; and this land becomes theirs from generation to generation for ever.'" (Skeen, Adam's Peak, p. 285.)—*B.*

† *Conacâr*—Dr. Lee identifies this place with Gampola, and he is followed by Pridham and Tennent. According to Turnour's Epitome, Gampola did not become the capital till after 1347, while Ibn Batúta is writing of the end of 1344. The Siṇhalese monarchy was then in a very troublous condition, and it is difficult to decide upon the locality of *Conacâr*.—[Skeen (Adam's Peak, p. 286) hesitates between Gampola and Ratnapura, the place where gems are chiefly found.] Col. Yule (Cathay, p. 423, Note) suggests that it was Kuruṇegala.

[Mr. L. Nell writes:—"Sir Emerson Tennent did not hesitate to identify this Sovereign with Bhuwanéka Báhu IV., whose capital was Gaṇgasripura, the modern Gampola. This identification was based on the Chronological Table of

of the principal Sovereign of the Island. It is built in a gully, between two mountains, near a great vale, called 'the vale of precious stones,'* because gems are found in it. Outside this town is seen the Mosque of the Shaikh *'Othmân* of Shiráz, surnamed *Châoûch (the usher)*. The King and inhabitants of the place visit him, and treat him with high consideration. He used

---

Turnour; but there are two grounds to doubt this identification. In the first place Turnour admitted an anachronism about A.D. 1347, the date assumed for the accession of Bhuwanéka Báhu IV, because the terms of three reigns immediately preceding this Sovereign are not given. Secondly, the capital of *Kinár* or *Konâr* is described as situate in a valley between two hills in a 'vale' (or according to Lee 'bay') in which gems were found. The term *Conacâr*, sounds like an Arab attempt to reproduce the name Kurunẹgala. Ibn Batúta wrote in A.D. 1344; according to Turnour, Gampola did not become the capital till after A.D. 1347. We are thus thrown back to a period before the accession of Bhuvanéka Báhu IV. There is an old native route between Puttaḷam and Kurunẹgala. The route from Puttaḷam to Gampola direct has not been known." The correspondent already quoted notes:—"In tracing the traveller beyond Chilaw reference is necessary to Ceylon history. Incomparably the best authority for this period is the *Nikáya Saṇgraha*, which was composed about 1396 A.D (Turnour states 1357 A.D., but that is manifestly wrong, as the author describes all the Kings up to Bhuvanaika Báhu V., who came to the throne 1914 A.B., showing Turnour's date to be wrong by 7 years): the corresponding portion of the *Mahâwaṇso* was written in 1758 A.D., and is not of anything like the same authority.

"The King of Siṇhalese Ceylon in 1344 A.D. was Bhuvanaika Báhu IV. He ascended the throne 1342 A.D., and did not move the seat of Government to Gampola from Kurunẹgala until 1346 A.D. Consequently *Conácar* must be (as indeed one would expect from the sound) Ibn Batúta's way of rendering Kurunẹgala. It lies 'between two mountains,' the Handrukkanda range and the Yakdessa range."—*B*.]

* "The valley of the Mahá-oya which is within 10 miles of Kurunẹgala. The word '*Manikam*' used by the traveller (Lee's version) occurs in two villages in this valley *Mẹnik-divela* and *Mẹnik-kaḍawara*. The valley was celebrated for precious stones (see *Kaḍaim pota*), and the latter was a place of some notoriety in the 16th century, and figures in Tennent's Portuguese map as *Manicávare*: it is near Polgahawela."—*B*.

to serve as a guide for those who go to see the Foot. When he had his hand and foot cut off, his sons and slaves became guides in his stead. The cause of his being so mutilated was that he killed a cow. Now the law of the Hindus ordains that one who has killed a cow should be massacred in like wise, or enclosed in its skin and burnt. The Shaikh *'Othmân* being respected by those people, they contented themselves with cutting off his hand and foot, and granted to him, as a present, the dues levied at a certain market.

OF THE SULTAN OF *CONACÂR*.

He is called by the name *Conâr*,* and possesses the white elephant. I have never seen in the world another white elephant. The King rides him on solemn occasions, and attaches to the forehead of this animal large jewels. It happened to this Monarch that the nobles of his empire rebelled against him, blinded him, and made his son King. As for him, he still lives in this town, deprived of his sight.

---

* *Conâr*—According to Turnour's list of Siṇhalese monarchs, the King at this time, 1344–45, would be Wijaya Báhu the Vth. Col. Yule (Cathay, p. 423 Note) thinks *Conâr* or *Kunâr* is the Sanskṛit *Kunwar*, 'prince.'

["Col. Yule's guess" adds Mr. Nell "at the name of the Sovereign *Conâr*,' as identical with '*Kunwar*,' the Sanskṛit for 'Prince', comes near what I conceive to be the fact. It will be seen that the Arab traveller describes a Mahommedan Mosque, outside the town of this Prince. Now, a Mahommedan Prince, *Vasthimi Kumaraya*, did reign with great popularity in Kuruṇegala. His romantic story is a local tradition in that town. He is said to have been treacherously murdered by the Buddhist priests of a temple on *Etágala*. They invited him to be present at a religious ceremony and suddenly pushed him over the precipice [Pridham, Vol. II., p. 649]. Offerings are made upon a mound on the road to the Máligáwa, which probably marks the spot where the Prince was interred, or the Shaikh referred to hereafter. No native will venture to pass the spot after dark without company, for the spirit of *Gala-Baṇḍára*, on horseback, is supposed to ride about the neighbourhood. The Court is said to have been immediately removed to Dambadeniya after this assassination, on the ground that the sanctity of the city had been polluted by a Mahommedan usurper.

Of the precious Stones.

The admirable gems called *albahramân (rubies or carbuncles)* are only found at this town. Some of them are found in the vale and these are the most precious in the eyes of the natives: others are extracted from the earth. Gems are met with in all localities in the island of Ceylon. In this country the whole of the soil is private property. An individual buys a portion of it, and digs to find gems. He comes across stones white-branched: in the interior of these stones the gem is hidden. The owner sends it to the lapidaries, who scrape it until it is separated from the stones which conceal it. There are the red (*rubies*), the yellow (*topazes*), and the blue (*sapphires*) which they call *neïlem* (nîlem).* It is a rule of the natives that precious stones whose value amounts to 100 fanams are reserved for the Sultan, who gives their price and takes them for himself. As for those of an inferior price, they remain the property of the finders.† One hundred fanams are equivalent to six pieces of gold.

It is probable that the priest, who compiled the history referred to by Turnour, has purposely omitted the name of this *Kumáraya*, thus causing the anachronism noticed by Turnour. Cásie Chetty conjectures that this Prince was the son of Wijaya Báhu V. by his Moorish Queen *Vasthimi* and this is quite consistent with the above theory. It is also stated by Ibn Batúta that the King and inhabitants of *Conacâr* used to visit the Mahommedan Shaikh *'Othmân* of Shiraz at his Mosque, and to treat him with great respect. It is significant that the Prince of *Conacâr* is not mentioned in the French translation as 'an infidel King', as Ibn Batúta seems to be careful to do in all instances of those who were not his co-religionist. The French translation also describes this King as deposed by his subjects and deprived of his sight, whilst his son was placed on the throne. This son may have been *Vasthimi Kumáraya*. The silence of the Siṃhalese historians has, however left all this in doubt."—*B.*]

* *Neïlem* = S. *nila*.

† Barbosa on the other hand says that all the Ceylon gemming is done by the agents of the King, and on his behalf. The stones are brought to him, and his lapidaries select the best, and sell the rest to the merchants (Stanley's

All the women in the island of Ceylon possess necklaces of precious stones of divers colors: they wear them also at their hands and feet, in the form of bracelets and *khalkhâls* (*anklets*). The concubines of the Sultan make a network of gems and wear it on their heads. I have seen on the forehead of the white elephant seven of these precious stones, each of which was larger than a hen's egg. I likewise saw in possession of *Aïry Chacarouaty* a ruby dish, as large as the palm of the hand, containing oil of aloes. I expressed my astonishment at this dish, but the Sultan said, "We have objects of the same material larger than that."*

We left *Conacâr*, and halted at a cave called by the name of *Ostha Mahmoûd Alloûry*. This person was one of the best of men: he had excavated this cave in the mountain side, near a little vale. Quitting this place, we encamped near the vale called *Khaour bouzneh* ('*monkey vale*'). *Bouzneh* (*Persian* boûzineh) designates the same as *alkoroûd* (*plural of* alkird, '*monkey*') in Arabic.

Of the Monkeys.

These animals are very numerous in the mountains: they are of a black colour, and have long tails. Those of the male sex have beards like men. The Shaikh '*Othmân*, his son and other persons, have related to me that the monkeys have a Chief whom they obey like a Sovereign. He binds round his head a wreath of the leaves of trees, and supports himself with a staff. Four

---

Barbosa, Hakt. Soc., p. 169.) Ludovico di Varthema (A.D. 1505) says :—"And when a merchant wishes to find these jewels, he is obliged first to speak to the King, and to purchase a *braza* of the said land in every direction (which *braza* is called a *molan* [? *amuṇam*], and to purchase it for five ducats. And then when he digs the said land, a man always remains there on the part of the King, and if any jewel be found there which exceeds ten carats, the King claims it for himself and leaves all the rest free."—Badger's Varthema, Hakt. Soc., p. 190.

* See further, as to the wonderful gems of that period, Marco Polo, Bk. III., Ch. xiv., and Col. Yule's note thereto.

monke s, bearing staves, march on his right and left, and, when the chief is seated, they stand behind him. His wife and little ones come and sit before him every day. The other monkeys come and squat at some distance from him: then one of the four above-mentioned gives them the word and they withdraw; after which, each brings a banana, or a lime, or some such fruit. The King of the monkeys, his little ones, and the four chief monkeys then eat. A certain *djogui* related to me that he had seen these four monkeys before their Chief, occupied in beating another monkey with a stick, after which they plucked his hair.*

Trustworthy persons have reported to me that when one of these monkeys has got possession of a young girl, she is unable to escape his lust. An inhabitant of the island of Ceylon has told me that he had a monkey, and when one of his daughters entered the house, the animal followed her. She cried him off, but he did her violence. "We ran to her aid," continued the speaker, "and seeing the monkey embracing her, we killed him."

Then we took our departure for 'the vale of bamboos,'† where *Abou 'Abd Allah*, son of *Khafíf*, found two rubies, which he

* "This is evidently a confused account of the Vęddás and their customs. Ibn Batúta was now in their country, *Sabaragamuwa*, through which he was journeying, being, as its name imports, 'the Vęddá village.'" (Skeen, *loc. cit.* p. 289). See C.A.S. Journ., Vol. VII., Pt. II., No. 24, 1881, p. 107.—*B.*

† "Passing through the forest, and cresting several hills that rose each higher than the one behind we came to Ali-hântenne, [Ali-hén-tęna] a tract of dense canes or *batali*, crossed in all directions by numerous elephant tracks. This was evidently one of the favourite feeding grounds of that monarch of the forest, as the name it bore plainly enough indicated. Beyond this is an extensive marsh, thickly covered with large reeds,—'the estuary of reeds' of Ibn Batúta, [Lee's version]—a swampy district, not at all pleasant to pass at any season, wet or dry, owing to the swarms of leeches that infest it: and further on is Baṭapola..... On the right of the path, in the upward ascent, is one of the caves which Ibn Batúta refers to in his narrative. It is formed by a straight fissure, in shape like an immense inverted V, running longitudinally through a huge boulder 40 feet in length, from 12 to 15 feet in height, and proportionally broad." (Skeen, *loc. cit.*, p. 146).—*B.*

presented to the Sultan of the Island, as we have related in the first part of these Voyages (*Tome II., p. 81*): then we marched to the place called ' the house of the old woman,'* which is at the extreme limit of the inhabited region. We left that for the cave of *Bâbâ Thâhir*, who was a good man; and then for that of *Sébîc*. This *Sébîc* was one of the idolater Sovereigns, and has retired to this spot to occupy himself with the practices of devotion.†

Of the Flying Leech.

At this place we saw the flying leech, by the natives called *zoloû*. It lives upon trees and herbs in the neighbourhood of water, and when a man approaches, it pounces upon him. Whatever be the part of the body upon which the leech falls, it draws therefrom much blood. The natives take care to have ready in that case a lime, the juice of which they express over

---

* "A steep and rough ascent, for a considerable distance from Baṭapola, —midway in which a stone tumulus has been erected on the spot where the remains of an old priest were burned—brings the pilgrim to Palábaddala, 'the house of the old woman,' according to Ibn Baṭúta, and 'the farthest inhabited part of the island of Ceylon' [Lee's version], that is, when he travelled through it, about five hundred and thirty years ago. * * * *

"The following legend is connected with the place, and accounts for its name:—Long, long ago, a very poor woman was desirous of performing the pilgrimage to the Ṣrí-páda, but, owing to her extreme poverty. could take nothing with her except some common jungle leaves, which in times of distress the natives occasionally resort to for food; these she boiled, and rolled up in a plaintain leaf; and having arrived thus far, when about to partake of her food, she found the boiled leaves had been miraculously turned into rice. Thenceforward it was called *Palá-bat-dola*, 'the place [rill] of rice and vegetables,' a name which it has ever since retained." (Skeen, *loc., cit.* p. 147, 154-5.)—*B.*

† "An ascent of some fifty feet brings the pilgrim to the crest of the ridge of which the Dharmma-rāja-gala forms a part. On the other side there is a rapid descent of some hundred and twenty feet, to the Gaṇgula-héna-ẹlla, midway to which is the Telihilena, a rocky cave, where tradition says an ancient King (? King Síbak), who had forsaken his throne for an ascetic life, took up his abode." (Skeen, *loc. cit.*, pp. 176-7.)—*B.*

the worm, and this detaches it from the body: they scrape the place with a wooden knife made for the purpose. It is said that a certain pilgrim was passing this neighbourhood, and that the leeches fastened upon him. He remained impassive, and did not squeeze lime-juice upon them: and so all his blood was sucked and he died.* The name of this man was *Bâbâ'Khoûzy*, and there is there a cave which bears his name. From this place we took our way to 'the seven caves,' then to 'the hill of Iskandar' (*Alexander*). There is there a grotto called of *Alisfahâny*, a spring of water, and an uninhabited mansion, beneath which is the bay called 'the place of bathing of the contemplative.' At the same place is seen 'the orange cave' and 'the cave of the Sultan.' Near the latter is the gateway (derwâzeh *in Persian*, bâb *in Arabic*) of the mountain.†

* Dr. Lee has this note :—"Knox describes these leeches as being rather troublesome than dangerous. His words are :—'There is a sort of leaches of the nature of ours, onely differing in colour and bigness; for they are of a dark reddish colour like the skin of bacon, and as big as a goose-quill; in length some two or three inches. At first, when they are young, they are no bigger than a horse-hair, so that they can scarce be seen. In dry weather none of them appear, but immediately upon the fall of rains, the grass and woods are full of them. These leaches seize upon the legs of travellers......Some, therefore, will tie a piece of *lemon* and salt in a rag, and fasten it unto a stick, and ever and anon strike it upon their legs to make the leaches drop off: others will scrape them off with a *reed, cut flat and sharp in the fashion of a knife*,' &c.—Ceylon, p. 25. See also the addition by Philalethes, p. 264." [*Zolon* = ? S. *kúdella*.—*B*.]

† "We had observed the preceding day, that from some place below the station [Heramitipána] on the side on which we entered it, coming from Palábaddala, the pilgrims brought up their supplies of water; and on returning from the Peak, in going down towards the Síta-gangula, we saw a descent to our left, which mistaking for the proper path, one of us went partially down before he discovered his error. About fifty or sixty feet below, he saw a clearing in a small dell, in the centre of which was a square kind of tank; and this dell he determined to examine on the occasion of his third visit. The result of the examination was, that he identified the station Heramitipána, and this place, as that described by Ibn Batúta as 'the ridge of Alexander, in which

OF THE MOUNTAIN OF SERENDIB (ADAM'S PEAK).

It is one of the highest mountains in the world: we saw it from the open sea, when we were distant from it upwards of nine days' march. While we were making the ascent, we saw the clouds above us, hiding from view the lower parts of it. There are upon this mountain many trees of kinds which do not cast their leaves, flowers of divers colors, and a red rose as large as the palm of the hand.* It is alleged that on this rose is an inscription in which one may read the name of God Most High and that of his Prophet.† On the mountain are two paths leading to the Foot of Adam. The one is known by the name of

---

is a cave and a well of water,' at the entrance to the mountain Serendib. The old Moor's account is somewhat confused, his notes or recollections not always carrying his facts exactly in their due order; but half way down the descent, on the left hand, is a well, excavated in the rock, in which we found about five feet of water, and which swarmed with tadpoles. Possibly Ibn Batúta found it in the same condition, for he speaks of the well, at the entrance, full of fish, of which 'no one takes any.' At the bottom of the dell is a cleared space; in the centre of this is a square tank or well, the sides of which are formed of blocks of stone, six or eight feet long. Beyond this, almost facing the descent, some twenty feet up the opposite mountain's side, is a cave. To this my companion and I forced our way through the jungle, and came to the conclusion that this was the cave of Khízr, where, Ibn Batúta says, the pilgrims leave their provisions, and whatever else they have, and then ascend about two miles to the top of the mountain, to the place of (Adam's) foot.' In the preceding sentence he says, 'Near this (cave) and on each side of the path, is a cistern cut in the rock.' Now, no other place that we saw, or heard of—and we were particularly minute in our inquiries—answers to such a description. There are the two wells, and the cave; and the distance to the foot-print is also pretty fairly estimated." (Skeen, *loc. cit.*, pp. 226-7.)—*B.*

* "Gigantic rhododendrons overhang the wall on the eastern side of the Peak. Their bending trunks seem, to the Buddhist mind, to bow to the foot-print; and to offer, in homage and adoration, their wealth of crowning crimson flowers to the pedal impress of the founder of their faith." (Skeen, *loc. cit.*, p. 200.).—*B.*

† The pious Musalmáns in this age of faith found their creed proclaimed by nature itself not only on the flowers of the rhododendron, but on the leaves

'the Father's path' and the other by that of 'the Mother's path. By these terms are Adam and Eve designated. The Mother's route is an easy one, and by it the pilgrims return; but any one who took it for the ascent would be regarded as not having done the pilgrimage. The Father's path is rough and difficult of ascent. At the foot of the mountain, at the place of the gateway, is a grotto also bearing the name of Iskandar, and a spring of water.

---

of the fig-tree. Before he went to the Máldives, Ibn Batúta was at *Deh Fattan* (? Dévipatam), a town on the Malabar Coast, where he records the existence of an extraordinary tree near the mosque. "I saw that the mosque was situated, near a verdant and beautiful tree; whose leaves resembled those of the fig, except that they were glossy. It was surrounded by a wall and had near it a niche or oratory, where I made a prayer of two genuflexions. The name of this tree with the natives of the country was *derakht* (dirakht) *acchêhâdah* 'the tree of the testimony.' I was informed at this place that every year, on the arrival of autumn, there fell from this tree a solitary leaf, whose colour passed first to yellow and then to red. On this leaf were written, with the pen of the Divine power, the words following 'There is no God but God, and Mohammed is the apostle of God.' The juris-consult *Houçain* and many other trustworthy men told me that they had seen this leaf, and had read the inscription upon it. *Houçain* added that, when the time arrived for it to fall, trusted men from among the Musalmáns and the idolaters sat down under the tree. When the leaf fell the Musalmáns took one half of it, while the other was deposited in the treasury of the idolater Sultan. The inhabitants preserve it for the purpose of curing the sick. This tree caused the conversion of the grandfather of *Coueïl* [the Sultan at the time of his visit] to the faith, and he it was who built the mosque and the tank [from its description similar to the Siṇhalese *pokuna*]. This prince could read the Arabic characters: and when he deciphered the inscription and understood what it contained, he embraced the true faith and professed it entirely. His story is preserved in tradition among the Hindús. The juris-consult *Houçain* told me that one of the children of this King returned to idolatry after the death of his father, governed with injustice, and ordered the tree to be torn up from the roots. The order was executed, and no vestige of the tree was left. Nevertheless it began to shoot again, and became as fair a tree as it had been before. As for the idolater, he came to die full soon thereafter." (Tome IV., pp. 85-87.) I have quoted this passage

The people of old have cut in the rock steps of a kind, by help of which you ascend; fixed into them are iron stanchions, to which are suspended chains, so that one making the ascent can hold on to them.* These chains are ten in number, thus:—two at the foot of the mountain [Peak] at the place of the gate-way; seven in contiguity after the two first; and the tenth, that is 'the chain of the profession of faith (*Islám*),' so named because a person who has reached it and looks back at the foot of the mountain will be seized with hallucinations, and, for fear of falling, he will recite the words "I bear witness that there is no God but God, and that Muhammad is his prophet." When you have passed this chain, you will find a path badly kept. From the tenth chain to 'the cave of *Khidhr*'† is seven miles. This cave is situate at an open place, and it has near it a spring of water full of fish, and this also bears the name of *Khidhr*. No one may catch these fish. Near the cave are two basins cut in the rock, one on each

at length as an illustration of the habit of missionary religions to annex and adapt the shrines and idols of local worship. The fig-tree in question was, I have little doubt, a *bó* tree, surrounded by a wall and altars like the *Mahá Viháré* at Anurádhapura. It is likely to have been credited with healing powers, and so to have preserved its influence in the locality from the decay of Buddhism in Malabar, through the centuries of Bráhmanish reaction, until at length the followers of the Prophet contrived by means of the fancied inscription to control the superstitious faith of its devotees. The similar attempt of the Muhammadans to annex the Ṣrí-páda of Samanala, by claiming it as the foot-print of Adam, has done nothing towards the conversion of the Siṇhalese. The Hindús claim it as that of Síva or Vishnu, according to their sect. (Skeen's Adam's Peak, p. 27.)

* These chains are spoken of by Marco Pólo in the previous century. "Furthermore you must know that on this Island of Seilan there is an exceeding high mountain; it rises right up so steep and precipitous that no one could ascend it, were it not that they have taken and fixed to it several great massive iron chains, so disposed that by help of these men are able to mount to the top."—Yule, Marco Polo, Vol. II., p. 256.

† See, as to the identity of this saint or prophet, Dr. Lee's note, and Sell, 'Faith of Islám,' p. 260.—*B.*

side of the path. In the grotto of *Khidhr* the pilgrims leave their belongings; thence they mount two miles further to the summit, where is the Foot.

DESCRIPTION OF THE FOOT.

The impression of the noble Foot, that of our father Adam, is observed in a black and lofty rock, in an open space. The Foot is sunk in the stone, in such wise that its site is quite depressed; its length is eleven spans.* The inhabitants of China came here formerly; they have cut out of the stone the mark of the great toe, and of that next to it, and have deposited this fragment in a temple of the town of *Zeïtoûn* (*Tseu-thoung*) whither men repair from the most distant provinces.† In the rock whereon is the print of the foot, are cut nine holes, in which the idolater pilgrims place gold, precious stones and pearls. You may see the fakírs, arrived from 'the grotto of *Khidhr*' seeking to get ahead of one another, and so to get what may be in these holes. In our case we found there only some little stones, and a

* Dr. Marshall, who in 1819 ascended the Peak with Mr. S. Sawers, says the foot is 5 ft. 6 in. in length. Tennent says it is "about 5 feet long, and of proportionate breadth" (Vol. II. p. 140), Knox (p. 3) says "about two feet long," but he never saw it. Ribeyro, Liv. i., C. xxiii., says, "two palms long and eight inches broad." See further Yule's Marco Polo, Vol. II., p. 261. Lieut. Malcolm, the first Englishman who made the ascent, (1815), says the impression is in kabook or ironstone. ["The heel is much higher than the toes, and the artificiality of the whole is palpable. A thick raised edging of cement marks the rude outline of a foot 5 ft. 7 in. long, and 2 ft. 7 in. broad at the point where the heel begins to curve. The interstices between the toes are also formed of cement, and the whole of the markings of the foot every now and again need repair. The inner portion of the heel and instep are the only parts that are clearly natural [gneiss] rock, (Skeen, *loc. cit.*, p. 203.)—*B.*]

† Marco Polo says that an embassy was sent by the great Khan in 1284 while he himself was in China, to obtain relics of our father Adam. They obtained a couple of teeth, some hair, and a dish of prophyry used by our first parent. He does not mention that they brought a piece of the rock from the foot-print.—Yule's Marco Polo, Vol. II., p. 259.

little gold which we gave to our guide. It is customary for pilgrims to pass three days in 'the cave of *Khidhr,*' and during this time to visit the Foot morning and evening: and so did we.

When the three days had elapsed, we returned by way of the Mother's path, and encamped hard by the grotto of *Cheîm,* who is the same as *Cheïth* (*Seth*) son of Adam. We halted in succession near 'the bay of fish,' the straggling villages of *Cermolah*, *Djeber-caouân*, *Dildînéoueh* and *Atkalendjeh.** It was in the last named place that the Shaikh *Abou 'Abd Allah,* son of *Khafîf* passed the winter. All these villages and stations are on the mountain. Near the base, on the same path, is the *dérakht* (dirakht) *rewân* 'the walking tree,' a tree of great age, not one of whose leaves falls. It is called by the name of *mâchïah (walking)* because a person looking at it from above the mountain considers it fixed a long distance off, and near the foot of the hill; while one who regards it from beneath, believes it to be in quite the opposite direction. I have seen at this place a b..nd

* [The correspondent before quoted writes:—"I fear the route taken by the traveller after leaving Kurunégala must always be a matter of conjecture. I have given it some attention and I think it most probable that he went from Kurunégala towards the mountains and ascended Adam's Peak from the pilgrim's path in Maskeliya. My reasons are—

(i.) The extreme limit of the inhabited region was evidently a long way from the Peak—this would be true on the Maskeliya side, but not true in the low country, as there were villages comparatively near the Peak.

(ii.) From the traveller's description he evidently went into the mountains soon after leaving Kurunégala.

(iii.) The names of places described are found on this route, and on no other.

(iv.) The traveller describes two routes as practicable. The 'father's path' as rough and difficult, the 'mother's path' as easy and the way of return. He went by the former, which is evidently the way through the hills and the forest of Maskeliya.

The most convenient pass from Kurunégala to the mountains runs past Girihágama, and there is a cave in the mountain side near a little vale (exactly as described) which still retains the name *Galagedara* ('cave abode').

of *djoguis,* who did not leave the foot of the hill, waiting for the fall of the leaves of this tree. It is planted in a place where there is no possibility of getting at it. The idolaters retail some fictions concerning it; among them, this—whoever eats of its leaves recovers his youth, even should he be an old man. But that is false.

Under this mountain is a great vale where precious stones are found. Its waters appears to the eye extremely blue. From this we marched for two days as far as the town of *Dînewer,* a large one, built near the sea and inhabited by merchants.* In a vast temple is seen an idol bearing the same name as the town. In this temple are upwards of a thousand Bráhmins and *djoguis,*

'Monkey vale' I cannot identify; there is a place in Doļosbágé called *Wanduru-mána* ('monkey measure').

'The vale of bamboos (or reeds)' I should guess to be *Rambukpiţiya* in Upper Bulatgama; it is of some antiquity and importance, and lies right on the road to Adam's Peak.

The spot where 'Abú Abd-Allah found his two rubies is probably even yet to be identified by the name *Męnik-hambantoţa* ('the gem ford of the foreign trader') on the pilgrim's route. 'The house of the old woman' (*A'chchi-gedara ?*)* has probably not survived till our time. The rest of the route lay through 'the wilderness of the Peak,' containing no inhabitants but hermits. The Royal hermit called *Sébîk* I should guess to be 'Raja Savlu (or Sakra) Vije Bahu,' afterwards father of the Şrí-Parákrama Báhu VI. (Valentyn, p. 71, and Kavya-sékara, 89.) Of the straggling villages mentioned as halting places on the journey to Dondra, *Cormolah* is probably Gilimalé; *Dildînéoueh* may be either Dinawaka or a Deldeniya; and *Atkalandjeh* is certainly the Atakalan Kóralé, the last district 'on the mountain' (*i.e.,* Kanda-uḍa or in the Uḍa-raṭa).

"The pass would probably be that traversed on the road from *Dápané* to *U'rubokka,* which is the beginning of 'the great vale [leading to Mátara] where precious stones are found. Its waters appear to the eye extremely blue'—of course the reference is to the *Nilwalá-gaṇga* ('blue-cloud-river')—and precious stones are still found there in some quantity (Cf. Pybus' Journey to Kandy, p. 22). *Dínewer* is of course Déwi-nuwara, and *Kâly,* Galle."—*B.*]

* *Dinéwar:*—Dondra. This magnificent shrine of Vishṇu was pillaged and destroyed by the Portuguese under Thomé de Souza d'Arronches in 1587. (De Couto, Dec. x., C. xv.)—Tennent 'Ceylon,' Vol. II., p. 113-4.

and about five hundred women, born of idolater fathers, who sing and dance every night before the statue. The town and its revenues are the private property of the idol; all who live in the temple and those who visit it are supported therefrom. The statue is of gold and of the size of a man. In place of eyes, it has two large rubies, and I was told that they shone by night like two lamps.

We took our departure for the town of *Kâly*,* a small one, six parasangs from *Dînewer*. A Musalman there, called the Ship-Captain *Ibrâhîm*, entertained us at his house. We then took the route for the town of *Calenbou (Colombo)* one of the largest and most beautiful in the island of *Sérendib*. There dwells the Vizier, prince of the sea, *Djâlesty*,† who has there about 500 Abyssinians. Three days after leaving *Calenbou*, we arrived at *Batthâlah*, of which mention is made above. We visited the Sultan of whom I have spoken. I found the Captain *Ibrâhîm* awaiting me, and we left for the country of *Ma'bar*.

[Ibn Batúta and his friends met with tempestuous weather, and were wrecked on the Coast of Coromandel, probably near the mouth of the Patar. He and his party, consisting of two concubines, some companions and slaves, were conducted to Arcot, and thence two days journey to the Sultan, who was engaged in an expedition against the infidels. This was the Sultan

---

* *Kâly*:—Galle. Six parasangs will be a little over 30 miles. The exact distance is 31·38 miles.

† *Djâlesty*:—This appears to be the same Prince described by the traveller John de Marignolli who was driven upon the coast of Ceylon on the 3rd May (probably) 1350. He landed at Perivilis (? Barberyn) "over against Paradise. Here a certain tyrant, by name *Coya Jaan*, a eunuch, had the mastery in opposition to the lawful king. He was an accursed Saracen, who, by means of his great treasures, had gained possession of the greater part of the kingdom." This person "in the politest manner" robbed him of the valuable gifts he was carrying home to the Pope, and detained him four months.—Yule's 'Cathay,' p. 357.

Ghiyâth eddîn, whose wife was a sister of a woman Ibn Batúta had married at Delhi: he is therefore above called his brother-in-law. Ibn Batuta was hospitably entertained, and he thus continues:—]

I had an interview with the Sultan and proposed the subject of the Máldives, and the sending of an army to the islands. He formed a resolve to accomplish this object, and appointed the ships for the purpose. He arranged a present for the Queen of Máldives, robes of honor, and gifts for the Emirs and Viziers. He entrusted to me the care of securing a marriage for him with the sister of the Queen; and lastly, he ordered three ships to be loaded with alms for the poor of the islands, and said to me, "You will get back in five days." The Admiral *Khodjah Serlec* said to him, "It will not be possible to go to the Máldives until three months from this moment." The Sultan went on to address me, "Since that is so, come to *Fattan*, so that we may finish this expedition and return to our capital at *Mouirah (Madura):* you will set out from there." I then remained with him, and as we waited I sent for my concubines and my comrades.

[*Ghiyâth eddîn* won a great victory over the infidels and returned with Ibn Batúta to *Fattan* (? Dévipatam) a large seaport town, and thence to Madura. At *Fattan* the Sultan told the Admiral to cease preparing the vessels for the Máldive expedition. He was then suffering from an illness, and shortly afterward died at a place near Madura. He left no son, and his nephew, *Nâssir eddîn*, whom Ibn Batúta had known as a domestic servant at Delhi, was accepted by the army, and reigned in his stead:—]

He [*Nâssir eddîn*] ordered that I should be provided with all the ships which his uncle had assigned to take me to the Máldives. But I was attacked with fever, which is mortal at this place. I imagined that I was about to die. God inspired me to have recourse to the tamarind, which is very abundant in that country: I took about a pound and put it in water. I then drank the beverage, and that relieved me in three days, and God healed me. I took a disgust for the town of *Moutrah,* and requested the Sultan's permission to take a voyage. He said, "Where would you go? There remains only a month ere you start for the Máldives. Remain here and we shall give you all the equipment ordered by the master of the world *(the deceased Sultan).*" I declined, and he wrote an order in my favor to *Fattan,* that I should be allowed to depart in any vessel I would. I returned to that town, and there found eight vessels setting sail for Yemen, and in one of them I embarked.

[Ibn Batúta left this ship at *Caoulem (Quilon)* on the Malabar Coast, and there remained for three months. He then embarked in another, which was attacked by the pirates near *Hinaour (Honore),* and the traveller lost all his property, including the pearls and precious stones presented to him by the Ceylon King, and all his clothes:—]

I returned to Calicut and entered one of the Mosques. A lawyer sent me a suit of clothes; the Kâzi, a turban, and a merchant, another coat. I was here informed of the marriage of the Vizier *'Abd Allah* with the Queen *Khadîdjah,* after the death of the Vizier *Djémâl eddîn,* and I heard that my wife, whom I had left *enceinte,* was delivered of a male child. It came into my heart to go back to the Máldives, but I feared the enmity which existed between me and the Vizier *A'bd Allah.* In consequence, I opened the Kuran, and these words appeared before me, "The angels shall descend unto them, and shall say, 'Fear not, neither be ye grieved.'" *(Kuran, Sur. xii., 30.)* I implored the benediction of God, took my departure, and arrived in ten days at the Máldives, and landed at the island of *Cannaloûs.* The Governor of this island, *'Abd al 'Azîz Almakdachâouy,* welcomed me with respect, entertained me, and got a barque ready. I arrived in due course at *Hololy,** an island to which the Queen and her sisters

* *Hololy* :—Probaly *Oluveli* island in North Mále Atol.—*B.*

resort for their diversion and for bathing. The natives term these amusements *tetdjer*,* and they then have games on board the vessels. The Vizier and chiefs send offerings to the Queen of such things as are found in the island. I met there the Queen's sister, wife of the preacher *Mohammed*, son of *Djémál eddin*, and his mother, who had been my wife. The preacher visited me, and he was served with food.

Meanwhile some of the inhabitants went across to the Vizier *'Abd Allah* and announced my arrival. He put some questions about me and the persons who had come with me, and was informed that I had come to take my son, who was now about two years old. The mother presented herself before the Vizier to complain of me, but he told her, "I will not prevent him taking away his son." He pressed me to go to the island *(Mahal)*, and lodged me in a house built opposite the tower of his Palace, in order that he might be aware of my estate. He sent me a complete suit of clothes, betel, and rose-water, according to custom. I took to him two pieces of silk to throw down at the moment of saluting him. These were received from me, with the intimation that the Vizier would not come out to receive me that day. My son was brought to me, and it seemed to me that a sojourn among the islanders was what was best for him. I, therefore, sent him back, and remained five days in the island. I thought it best to hasten my departure, and asked the usual permission. The Vizier sent for me and I repaired to his presence. They brought to me the two pieces of stuff they had previously taken from me, and I cast them before the Vizier and saluted him in the customary way. He made me sit by his side and questioned me of my condition. I ate in his company and washed my hands in the same basin with him, which thing he does with no one. Then betel was brought and I came away. The Vizier sent me

---

* *Tetdjer*:—Cf. M. *kuli-jahan* 'sports.'—*B.*

cloths and *bostoûs* of cowries, and conducted himself towards me in the most perfect way. I took my departure and after a voyage of forty-three days we arrived at Bengal.

[The son of Ibn Batuta here spoken of was probably born before the close of 1344. The traveller therefore took his final departure from the Máldives about the close of the year 1346.]